Blending Instruction with Technology

D1457897

Blending Instruction with Technology

A Blueprint for Teachers to Create Unique, Engaging, and Effective Learning Experiences

Michael Martin

ROWMAN & LITTLEFIELD
Lanham • Boulder • New York • London

Published by Rowman & Littlefield
A wholly owned subsidiary of The Rowman & Littlefield Publishing Group, Inc.
4501 Forbes Boulevard, Suite 200, Lanham, Maryland 20706
www.rowman.com

Unit A, Whitacre Mews, 26-34 Stannary Street, London SE11 4AB

British Library Cataloguing in Publication Information Available

Library of Congress Cataloging-in-Publication Data
Names: Martin, Michael, 1974– author.
Title: Blending instruction with technology : a blueprint for teachers to create
    unique, engaging, and effective learning experiences / Michael Martin.
Description: Lanham : Rowman & Littlefield, [2016] | Includes bibliographical
    references and index.
Identifiers: LCCN 2016010399 (print) | LCCN 2016017153 (ebook) | ISBN
    9781475826999 (cloth : alk. paper) | ISBN 9781475827002 (pbk. : alk. paper) |
    ISBN 9781475827019 (Electronic)
Subjects: LCSH: Blended learning. | Educational technology. | Education—
    Effect of technological innovations on.
Classification: LCC LB1028.5 .M325 2016 (print) | LCC LB1028.5 (ebook) | DDC
    371.33—dc23
LC record available at https://lccn.loc.gov/2016010399

∞™ The paper used in this publication meets the minimum requirements of
American National Standard for Information Sciences—Permanence of Paper
for Printed Library Materials, ANSI/NISO Z39.48-1992.

Printed in the United States of America

The dogmas of the quiet past are inadequate to the stormy present. The occasion is piled high with difficulty, and we must rise with the occasion. As our case is new, so we must think anew and act anew. We must disenthrall ourselves and then we shall save our country.

—Abraham Lincoln

Contents

Preface

It was one of those moments where every hair on your neck stands up. As an educator, it is the rare but surreal moment that justifies why we join the education profession. Riley, a fifth-grader, is standing in anticipation as he watches the teacher and a few of the high school students enter his fifth-grade room. Riley was born without a hand. He has spent his entire life with either only one hand or one hand and a prosthetic. As the teacher and students unveil the prosthetic hand they had designed and printed on a three-dimensional printer, Riley, ravaged with excitement and emotions, begins to run in place. It is one of those moments that would drive anybody with a heartbeat to tears.

It is truly amazing how, in 2014, a group of determined and well-intentioned high school students led by an amazing teacher can create a prosthetic hand. What is more, the hand is usable and due to the low cost (just under $30) the hand can be reprinted each year as Riley grows. Technology in the classroom can be such a powerful tool.

Therein lies the fundamental purpose of this book. Technology is and always will be a tool. Technology cannot and will not supersede the classroom instructor. That being said, a teacher alone, one without technology, is behind the eight ball. This is due to the great advances in technology as well as technology's affordable prices. Teaching and learning now go hand in hand with technology.

Sadly, not many educators truly understand what teaching with technology really means. I have been afforded the opportunity to witness many well-educated and good-intentioned teachers fall victim to technology's fatal flaws.

Flaw 1: Schools believe a good use of technology is to create a wireless infrastructure that would allow students to "Bring Your Own Device" (BYOD). Teachers then would allow students to use their devices to look up answers to questions the class did not know. This is an all too common strategy. Is this good teaching? Is this using technology to enhance education? In this case, isn't the device really only replacing a textbook? Instead of having students look up the answer in a textbook, the teacher allows the students to use their devices.

Flaw 2: I have seen too many educators preach they are teaching twenty-first-century skills. Please understand I fully believe that we need to not only teach twenty-first-century skills but our students should also be immersed in them.

So where's the flaw here? Here is a list of some of the twenty-first-century skills our students may encounter:

- QR codes
- Doceri
- Reflector
- Socrative
- Prezi
- Animoto
- Poster Maker
- Glogster
- Educreations
- Voki
- GAFE (Google Apps for Education)

Does this look like a list of skills? More accurately, this is a list of web-based tools. Granted, these are some really unique and powerful web-based tools, but they are not skills. Far too many times I have witnessed well-intentioned and good teachers refer to these as twenty-first-century skills.

Let me make this point very clear; the list above includes tools to engage the twenty-first-century student, these are not *twenty-first-century skills*!

This is the message at the heart of this book. This book will serve as a beginning to understand how to enhance education. It will introduce educators to multiple web-based tools. It will also provide school leaders (principals, curriculum directors, instructional coaches, etc.) a framework with which to plan and initiate professional development that will meet educators where they are and move them forward.

The book will allow educators time to reflect on their teaching. It will provide examples on how to use these web-based tools in the classroom. You will be asked to pinpoint areas of weakness in your instruction method and then be provided multiple digital tools to improve these areas.

Again, it is important to note, this book will walk educators and school leaders through planning and using technology as a tool to enhance education. *This book does not replace the teacher with technology.* This book firmly places the teacher at the heart of education as the driver of high-quality classroom instruction.

To reach this end, you will be exposed to fundamental frameworks of cognitive development such as Bloom's Revised Taxonomy and Webb's Depth of Knowledge. You will also be provided with examples of teachers using technology as a tool to provide learning opportunities that take advantage of both of these cognitive development theories.

Hopefully, the educators reading this book will not only be provided with insights on how to use the tool of technology as a way to facilitate good teaching, but they will also be inspired to continue to learn and grow. As educators increase their knowledge and confidence, the result will be engaged students and improved student achievement.

Acknowledgments

Where to start? There are so many people I owe so much to. Much of my current success is due to the many blessings that I have received from others along the way. Truly, if for some reason I have a different view of education than others, it is because I have stood on the shoulders of giants. To those Giants I say thank you. Thank you for your tutelage. Thank you for your patience. Thank you for your kindness. Thank you for your wisdom. Most importantly, thank you for believing in me, even when others didn't.

My Giants: Mrs. Picchocki, Mrs. McDiffitt, George Wechter, Glen Guttenberg, Mike Tracy, Dr. Hogan, Dr. Stein, John Hill, Dr. Theresa Schaffer, Greg Noftz, Roger Jury, Dr. Jim Metcalf, John Swese, Dr. Greg Gerrick, Dr. Ann Shelly, Dr. Harold Wilson, Dr. Howard Walters, all of Cohort X, Greg Nickoli, and Glenna Cannon.

Also, a special thank you to Sarah Jubar, none of this would be possible without you. Thank you for seeing the potential in this work. Thank you for providing guidance while I was writing this book. You have done more than your job—you have touched lives!

Most importantly, thank you to my family. The completion of this book is a culmination of family influences on my life. My mother, father, stepmother, stepfather have all played a critical role in my development. My sisters Deb, Amanda, Katie, and my little brother Rich. Also, my older brother, Rob, for always (I mean ALWAYS) believing in me. Never doubting my potential and serving as an unending source of positive support. He has always been the quiet hero in my life.

To my wife and kids. To whom all of this is for. Thank you for being the wonderful chaos that you are! Your joy and enthusiasm for life, while exhausting, is what motivates me during those long nights. I hope and pray that my (and your mother's) commitment to making the world better inspires you to do the same. I hope and pray that this work has a positive impact on your educational experiences. Always remember, you are my greatest accomplishment.

And to all of the educators out there. Thank you for being my inspiration each and every day!

Introduction

Today's education environment is laden with federal and state mandates coupled with multiple initiatives enacted by the administration or school board. Due to these, teachers are overwhelmed with all of the work that goes into each of these initiatives and mandates. If that were not enough, educators are tasked with educating each individual child, dealing with the complexities of the human mind, taking on the challenges of socioeconomic demographics, and interpreting multiple forms of data, to name a few. In short, teachers are doing all they can to keep their heads above water.

The answer to many of these issues is to use technology. Technology can play a critical role in providing individual education, meeting the students where they are, providing and interpreting data, as well as creating an environment that is inclusive to who the students are and to the world they live in.

That being said, this is yet another initiative for educators to tackle. What are the available tools that educators can use? How does one use those tools? Where do schools and educators find the time to provide professional development for these tools? Can schools provide a digital device? If so, is it sustainable? And maybe most importantly, just how does one go about teaching in a blended environment?

This book looks to tackle many of these questions. It provides a rationale for technology integration, a call for the need to integrate twenty-first-century skills, a model of cognitive consumption, a model of technology integration, a list of digital tools that meet the model of technology integration, as well as being a professional development guide.

TEXT ORGANIZATION

Chapter 1: Schools and Classrooms Are Becoming Dangerously Irrelevant

Drawing on Scott McLeod's blog "Dangerously Irrelevant," Chapter 1 describes the need for infusing technology in an effective and efficient classroom delivery system. The chapter illustrates the need by using the classic tale of Rip Van Winkle, Pew Research, an in-depth look at data using NextGen graphics, specific student quotes, current school reform vignettes, Future Ready Schools and Future Ready Students initiatives, as well as current social science from renowned author Dan Pink's perspective. It is an enlightening yet entertaining chapter that boldly pronounces the need for schools to move to a blended environment.

Chapter 2: Blended Learning . . .? Why?

Chapter 2 will dive deeper into the need for using technology in the classroom. This chapter will also define what blended learning is. To help illustrate this book's definition of a blended classroom, this chapter will compare and contrast the blended learning environment with the flipped classroom.

Chapter 3: Skill vs. Tools: The Classic Debate of the Chicken and the Egg

Chapter 3 will focus on a growing issue that has been observed during many visits to different schools as well as many conference sessions around the nation. That is, there seems to be confusion between twenty-first-century skills and twenty-first-century tools. Many educators seem to think that by simply using one of the many twenty-first-century digital tools that they are also teaching a twenty-first-century skill. That simply is not the case.

This chapter suggests that many of these tools are designed to promote collaboration; however, there is a difference between accidental collaboration and specifically planning for one of the many different twenty-first-century skills. This chapter will provide a brief introduction to the twenty-first-century skills and an explanation of what should come first when planning a twenty-first-century lesson—the skill or the tool?

Chapter 4: Twenty-First-Century Skills and Twenty-First-Century Classrooms

Chapter 4 will dive deeper into the twenty-first-century skills. The chapter will provide a rationale for the need of each specific skill and provide insights into multiple organizations' definition or description of twenty-first-century skills. The chapter will then focus on Partnership for 21st Century Learning (P21) as the main organizational driver of twenty-first-century skills and will offer multiple illustrations of these skills in the classroom.

Chapter 5: Skills Are Important, but Shouldn't Kids Think? Cognitive Models for Student Achievement

Chapter 5 provides insight into the absolute need to incorporate cognitive skills into each lesson. The chapter will provide two models to do so: Bloom's Revised Taxonomy and Webb's Depth of Knowledge. The chapter will also provide examples as illustrations.

Chapter 6: Stumbling Down the Right Path

Many schools have attempted the path to a blended learning environment. To be sure, some have been successful, but the research shows that most have not. Also, the research shows that there are some generalizable lessons that schools can use to help establish an effective path toward a blended environment. That being said, many lessons can be extrapolated from what schools have done wrong.

Chapter 6 will focus on the stumbling blocks that schools have encountered and will help the reader create a path by knowing what not to do, using known stumbling blocks to create the right path. The chapter will be filled with vignettes to help illustrate the stumbling blocks.

Chapter 7: ART: A Three-Step Process to Blended Learning

This chapter will dive into the known models that explain digital use in the classroom: RAT, SAMR, and TPACK. The chapter will explain each model, provide its pros and cons, and then focus on the Martin model of technology integration known as ART. The chapter will provide a rationale, as well as a diagnostic tool, for identifying where teachers fall within the ART model.

Chapter 8: Three-Stage Process to the ART of Blended Learning

This chapter will provide a detailed explanation to each of the three stages of the ART (Acclimate, Redesign, and Transfigure) of the blended learning process so schools can meet teachers where they are in regard to blended instruction and then move them forward. The chapter will provide digital tools, and summaries of each, that teachers can use for each stage. The chapter will provide a lesson plan detailing how to implement the tool to fit each specific stage and how to incorporate specific twenty-first-century skills as well as cognitive skills.

Chapter 9: Planning Tips

This chapter will provide illustrations of what happens to schools when they do not properly plan for the transition to a blended or one-to-one environment. The chapter will also highlight well-known research that contributes to high-quality professional development. Lastly, the chapter will provide an outline for high-quality professional development to help schools prepare for the blended learning transition.

Chapter 10: A Word of Caution

This chapter provides a philosophical word of caution for all schools and organizations regarding the use of digital devices. To help illustrate this, Chapter 10 will use George Orwell's *1984*, Aldous Huxley's *A Brave New World*, and Neil Postman's *Amusing Ourselves to Death*. The chapter considers, as a society, if we are amusing ourselves to death, especially in the classroom.

1

✛

Schools and Classrooms Are Becoming Dangerously Irrelevant

Scott McLeod, co-creator of the widely popular YouTube sensation "Did You Know? (Shift Happens)," created a blog titled "Dangerously Irrelevant." The blog is intended to engage readers in a multitude of technology-related issues in both the classroom and leadership. McLeod asserts that if schools continue on the path they currently are projected, it will not be long until we are irrelevant (Dangerously Irrelevant 2015).

Salman Khan, creator of the very successful Khan Academy, was recently interviewed by Big Think, an online bank of knowledge comprised from over 2,000 Big Think Fellows. In that interview he states: "There's this illusion that is created in our classical education system and even at university that someone is teaching it to you. Really they're creating a context in which you need to pull information and own it yourself" (You Are the Essence of Learning, Not a School or University, Big Think, 2015).

Khan Academy is a wonderful example of how innovators in education are disrupting the education process. There are illustrations of innovation all around us. As stated earlier, Khan Academy has changed education, so has Apple, Google, Promethean, and a host of other organizations. What each of these organizations has in common is their ability to leverage technology to create high-quality, on-demand, personalized education. And as McLeod asserts, this is making schools dangerously irrelevant.

If innovators are leveraging technology to create high-quality, on-demand, personalized education, than what are our schools doing? The answer, sadly, is the same thing they have been doing since the 1800s. To illustrate this point, let's revisit a very popular American story.

In a pleasant village, at the foot of New York's Catskill Mountains, lives the kindly Rip Van Winkle, a colonial British American villager of Dutch descent. Rip is an amiable man who enjoys solitary activities in the wilderness, but is also loved by all in town—especially the children to whom he tells stories and gives toys. However, a tendency to avoid all gainful labor, for which his nagging wife chastises him, allows his home and farm to fall into disarray due to his lazy neglect.

One autumn day, Rip is escaping his wife's nagging, wandering up the mountains with his dog, Wolf. Hearing his name being shouted, Rip discovers that the speaker is a man dressed in antiquated Dutch clothing, carrying a keg up the mountain, who requires Rip's help. Without exchanging words, the two hike up to a hollow in which Rip discovers the source of previously heard thunderous noises: there is a group of other ornately dressed, silent, bearded men who are playing nine-pins. Although there is no conversation and Rip does not ask the men who they are or how they know his name, he discreetly begins to drink some of their liquor and soon falls asleep.

He awakes in unusual circumstances: It seems to be morning, his gun is rotted and rusty, his beard has grown a foot long, and Wolf is nowhere to be found. Rip returns to his village where he finds that he recognizes no one. Asking around, he discovers that his wife has died and that his close friends have died in a war or gone somewhere else. He immediately gets into trouble when he proclaims himself a loyal subject of King George III, not knowing that the American Revolution has taken place; George III's portrait on the town inn has been replaced by that of George Washington. Rip is also disturbed to find another man is being called Rip Van Winkle (though this is in fact his son, who has now grown up) (Irving and Noyik, 1923).

Many people compare the story of Rip Van Winkle to "modern" schools. If Rip were alive today, the only place in the United States he would recognize is our schools. (For a short animated video of this popular belief, go to the website http://creatinglifelonglearners.com/?p=289.)

Schools would be the only place that Rip would recognize and feel comfortable in. Even with all of the technological disruption that has taken place over the past two decades, schools still have not moved to change how education is delivered. Despite the lives that our students live, the world they engage in, and the devices they use, schools have not moved to meaningfully adapt. Due to this, schools are on the brink of being dangerously irrelevant.

WHAT DO TWENTY-FIRST-CENTURY STUDENTS DO/USE?

In 2013 Pew Research completed a comprehensive survey on teens and their use of technology. The findings help us understand what our students are doing each and every day of their lives. Specifically, the impact of the smartphone has had tremendous effects (Teens and Technology, Pew Research Center, 2013): One in four teens are "cell-mostly" Internet users, who say they mostly go online using their phone and not using some other device such as a desktop or laptop computer. The study shows that:

- About three in four (74 percent) teens ages twelve to seventeen say they access the Internet on cell phones, tablets, and other mobile devices at least occasionally.
- One in four teens are "cell-mostly" Internet users—far more than the 15 percent of adults who are cell-mostly. Among teen smartphone owners, half are cell-mostly.
- Older girls are especially likely to be cell-mostly Internet users; 34 percent of teen girls ages fourteen to seventeen say they mostly go online using their cell phone, compared with 24 percent of teen boys ages fourteen to seventeen. This is notable since boys and girls are equally likely to be smartphone owners.
- Among older teen girls who are smartphone owners, 55 percent say they use the Internet mostly from their phone (Teens and Technology, Pew Research Center, 2013).

The research further illustrates:

- One in four teens (23 percent) have a tablet computer, a level comparable to the general adult population.
- Nine in ten (93 percent) teens have a computer or have access to one at home. Seven in ten (71 percent) teens with home computer access say the laptop or desktop they use most often is one they share with other family members (Teens and Technology, Pew Research Center, 2013).

In other words, most of our students, due to their own personal digital devices or their home devices, are powered up. They are online, they are communicating, consuming multiple modes of media. They are networking, they are socializing, and, yes, they are learning. This is just a small snapshot of who they are and what they do.

It is important that educators remember that the students in the hallways today have never known a world without a digital device. They have no memory of the past century, the same one that most of the teachers across America lived during and were educated in (Learning with "e's," 2015). This makes them residents of the digital age and the connected age. Also, they carry the equipment and capability for connection in their pocket every day (Learning with "e's," 2015).

That being said, when these same individuals come to our schools, we have them power down. We take them out of their natural environment and force them to be successful in ours. What is the impact of this forced lifestyle migration for eight hours a day, 180 days of the year? If you ask, they will tell you.

Grant Wiggins, a national leader in education reform, did just that. In a blog called "The Student Voice," he surveyed today's students. One of his survey questions was, "What is a very common teacher practice that occurs all the time in class but just does not work for you?" The responses to this question are very enlightening (Wiggins, 2011):

- Taking notes off the projector and it doesn't work because it doesn't help me to understand and take it in if I am just mindlessly writing down notes.
- Reading to me does not work for me.
- Lecturing, it's boring for the students and most people tend to zone out and not pay attention anyway.
- "Busy work!" In Spanish we read sections out of our book that do not help me learn. The book does not help prepare us for tests or finals and it makes the teacher seem lazy for not preparing anything better for us.
- Repetitive homework. More of the Same (MOTS). Teachers feel the need to assign for me, MOTS is just monotonous busy-work. It is literally just more of the same . . . very similar homework over and over again. This may help some students, however.
- I don't like it when a teacher just talks all period without some kind of visual or anything. It's very boring and I fall asleep all the time.
- Some teachers just read and have us write notes off PowerPoints.
- Getting a packet, read the book and find answers then finish it for homework. Instead of understanding what it is.
- The "Here's a packet teach yourself then take a test on it" method.
- Lectures do not work for me at all. I am a visual learner! Respect it! I think teachers should teach to every student's learning ways such as auditory and visual learners.
- Just simply when a teacher continues to write down notes on the board and the students spend the whole class time writing them down. We don't learn anything this way, just some basic facts if that.

The student input illustrates my point: when teachers spend all their time talking and students spend all their time writing, students are bored! Yet this seems to be a common teaching strategy across our nation.

It also reminds me of how I was taught. Rip Van Winkle would recognize this form of education. Heck, he might apply for a job and be hired. He would fit in well with many educators across the nation. Schools are on the brink of becoming dangerously irrelevant.

WHY WE NEED TO CHANGE!

As mentioned earlier, there have been many innovations and disruptions in education since Rip Van Winkle fell asleep. Schools are still using the same modes of education that were excitingly new in the twentieth century. Education environments, for the most part, are created by and for the providers (teachers) and not the consumers (students). This needs to change before schools become dangerously irrelevant.

As with any issue in education, there are some pockets of success. There are some schools that have managed to implement a blended environment that fits the needs of their students. These places have been successful. We can learn from these pockets of success. Burlington High School in Burlington, Massachusetts, implemented a one-to-one initiative using iPads for the 2011 school year. Below are great examples of technology use in the classroom (Edutopia, 2015):

1. French IV: A French IV class that was reading a detective novel was given an assignment to make a video of their favorite chapter. To complete this, the students used an application called VidEditor and then uploaded it to the class YouTube channel.
2. Calculus: A calculus class was given the task of teaching a lesson via a music video. To reach this end, the class filmed the video on iPads and completed the editing process using iMovie. Each group wrote a script and storyboard for the video and eventually presented it to the class.

These are just two examples from one successful school. Thousands of examples abound that illustrate this point. What these schools and classroom teachers are doing is creating learning environments that engage students to research, brainstorm, collaborate, network, analyze, synthesize, share, and create while using the tools our students naturally engage in as well as introducing students to new and more robust tools.

These schools are radically different from the ones that Rip Van Winkle attended. These schools are breaking the curve toward being dangerously irrelevant. As innovative as these schools are, the lessons still come up short. For example, review the lesson by Brighid Boyle earlier in the chapter. Certainly one would find it difficult to imagine the students were not engaged. I also believe students were utilizing multiple twenty-first-century tools to learn twenty-first-century skills. However, are the students more proficient at calculus because of this? What level of cognitive challenge and rigor exists to push students? Even the most innovative and glorified schools have much to learn and many areas to improve regarding high-quality blended learning.

DOES IT WORK?

The question many antagonists ask about including technology in the classroom is "Does this technology really help students learn? Does it improve student achievement?"

With a simple Google search one may become confused about the impact technology can have on student achievement. There are multiple studies that would indicate there is no impact. On the other hand, there are just as many studies that will cite student achievement gains due to technology. To help the average reader sift through the malaise of confusing information, let me point out some important search factors:

- Look for studies done in the past few years. Efficient use of technology and training has improved over time, allowing for better classroom technology integration.
- Look for studies that also emphasize schools that have properly prepared (e.g., planning, purchasing the proper device, whole school acceptance, and high-quality professional development before implementation).
- Look for studies that have multiple points of data and that take place over a period of time.

When inserting factors like this into the search, the findings for student achievement become both more positive and robust. Certainly, as researchers, the issue has been around but the literature of quality studies of quality programs is still fairly new. That being said, the results are exciting and encouraging. For example, Project Tomorrow (2015), found that:

- Nearly 50 percent of students in virtual schools report being interested in learning versus 32 percent in traditional schools.
- Seventy-four percent of teachers believe technology increases student engagement in the classroom.

- Technology is more impactful when used to support instruction rather than provide direct instruction. In and of itself, technology is purely another medium for helping propel students along their learning paths. But it can be used in a wide variety of ways.
- The International Society for Technology in Education (ISTE) policy brief offers a wealth of information such as, "Looking at the effect of technology in raising achievement in specific subject areas, of 11 studies published since 2000 assessing technology integration and mathematics achievement, seven showed strong positive effects on scores among elementary and secondary students" (DreamBox Learning, 2014).
- The U.S. Department of Education completed a systematic and comprehensive meta-analysis of the literature from 1996 to 2008. The report concludes that more than 1,000 empirical studies of online learning found a positive performance resulting from the use of technology (DreamBox Learning, 2014).
- A study titled Speak Up 2014 by Project Tomorrow found 40 percent of students are finding online videos to help with their homework and 28 percent say they regularly watch videos created by their teachers. Students are regularly using digital tools outside of school to communicate with their teachers (48 percent by e-mail and 16 percent by texting). Seventy-five percent of students think every student should have access to a mobile device during the school day to support learning; 58 percent are using their own smartphone and 47 percent are taking photos of class assignments or textbook pages (Project Tomorrow, 2015).

There is evidence to support the claim that technology, when implemented by educators who have prepared and trained to use it effectively, can impact student achievement. For example, Dr. Mark Edwards, superintendent of Mooresville Graded School District, in Mooresville, North Carolina, initiated a 1:1 movement. Edwards came to the district with technology integration experience and an enthusiasm for proper integration. The academic by-product of the movement is significant: between 2006 and 2012, the overall district achievement increased from 73 percent to 89 percent, third-grade math scores increased from 80 percent to 95 percent, biology scores increased from 70 percent to 95 percent, graduation rate increased from 94 percent to 97 percent, and scholarships earned increased from $935,370 to $2,685,583 (Edwards, 2014).

There are other factors to address besides student achievement. Technology has the ability to provide students with learning opportunities that will teach them twenty-first-century skills. Technology provides students the chance to learn on demand in any environment. Technology allows the teacher to assess students and receive immediate feedback and data. These data can and should be used to drive instruction.

Currently, there is a move to label this type of educational environment as a Future Ready Schools and Future Ready Students. Future Ready is a movement to prepare schools and students for (Future Ready School, 2014):

R: Robust and rigorous resources
E: Engaged students with equitable access
A: Active parents for deeper engagement
D: Dedicated educators
Y: "Yes culture" of leadership

An individual who is helping to spearhead this movement is Kevin Brookhouser, a teacher who has created an educational environment formulated around Dan Pink's bestselling book *Drive*.

In the book, Pink discusses an idea from Google called 20 percent time (Pink, 2009). The idea is to allow individuals to spend 20 percent of their time on projects they are excited and engaged to start, create, and complete. Kevin Brookhouser has brought this element to his class. He provides students 20 percent time to work on a real-world, individual, meaningful project.

By the end of the year each student needs to create a blog on his or her project, create an elevator pitch for their project, and present in front of the school's student population in a TED-style format. Each student also has to create a tangible product for his or her project. This is a great example of an educational environment that is engaging, individualized, rigorous, on-demand, thought-provoking, and community-oriented, utilizing twenty-first-century skills integrated with the appropriate technology (Brookhouser, n.d.). Education, delivered in this format, is extremely relevant.

So when the limited research results are coupled with what we know technology can do for both the student and the teacher, it is imperative that schools aggressively pursue a technology integration plan, because, as stated earlier, schools are on the brink of becoming dangerously irrelevant.

2

✛

Blended Learning? Why?

Here I will dive deeper into the need for using technology in the classroom. This chapter will also define what blended learning is. To help illustrate the definition of a blended classroom, this chapter will compare and contrast the blended learning environment with the flipped classroom.

As Chapter 1 pointed out, there is a definite need for schools to embrace the digital tools that are native to our students; otherwise, schools risk the chance of becoming dangerously irrelevant. Students are using these devices in their everyday lives, and these devices have so much potential to impact student achievement, yet schools, reluctantly, are slow to change in incorporating their use. This change needs to occur.

DEFINING BLENDED LEARNING:
BRICK MORTAR VERSUS CLICK AND MORTAR

As stated in Chapter 1, technology integration is difficult to define due to the various ways technology is used and the fast-paced change of technology. For purposes of this book, I will look to define the term by analyzing the foremost think tank on the subject, the Clayton Christensen Institute for Disruptive Innovation. According to the Clayton Institute, blended learning is "a formal education program in which a student learns:

1. at least in part through online learning, with some element of student control over time, place, path, and/or pace;

2. at least in part in a supervised brick-and-mortar location away from home;
3. and the modalities along each student's learning path within a course or subject are connected to provide an integrated learning experience" (Christensen Institute, 2015).

This definition formalized blended learning based on student control via time, place, path, and pace, and the location of educational services. Blended learning experiences do not occur in a vacuum; rather they are integrated through multiple modalities to create a specific learning experience. In short, *blended learning is a multimodal learning experience specifically crafted by the teacher to provide an integrated learning experience that will allow the learner (student) partial control over when, where, and how he or she will learn.* Within this model of education the delivery of instruction no longer occurs in a brick-and-mortar setting but rather in a "click-and-mortar" setting.

While the aforementioned definition is useful and will be used to operationalize the concept of blended learning, there are some distinct differences that should be pointed out to clarify this book's view of blended learning. Blended learning, to be as impactful as it can be, should ensure that the teacher remains the content expert and instructional leader of the classroom. The device and digital tool of choice is nothing more than a tool for the teacher. While blended learning certainly does provide an opportunity for students to have some control over when, where, and how they learn, it should play a supplemental role to the educator. Therefore, the majority of the instruction should occur during class time with the supervision of the classroom and content expert.

To further illustrate this point, a research article published by the Harvard Kennedy School found that between parents, blended learning experts, and teachers, roughly 30 percent of a school day (or classroom period) should be devoted to digital or online learning to be effective (Peterson and Horn, 2016), thus supporting the notion that highly effective blended learning should incorporate classroom and digital time.

Blended learning is more about the classroom environment than student control. Certainly there are times when the tool will be used outside the classroom. For example, students can and should use their devices and multiple learning tools for intervention purposes. This should be done in concert with the teacher. Their devices and digital tools should be used for enrichment opportunities that take place outside the classroom, but not on a consistent basis. Certainly, devices and digital tools should be used for extended and abstract learning opportunities outside the classroom as well, but again, this typically isn't the main mode of instructional delivery.

Other than the student, the teacher is still the most important variable in high-quality education. Therefore, the majority of learning should take place with the instructor. The instructor must have the ability to create a blended classroom environment and to engage the student. The core of blended learning should take place during designated classroom instructional time, and student control (when, where, and how) should serve as an academic supplemental opportunity.

BLENDED VS. FLIPPED

Aren't blended learning and the flipped classroom the same things? While many intelligent people will attempt to make the argument that they are, this book makes the claim that they are not. First, understand that the flipped classroom is a *form* of blended learning.

The flipped classroom doesn't fit the model or definition that was provided at the beginning of this chapter. Recall the book's short definition of blended learning, "Blended learning is a multimodal learning experience specifically crafted by the teacher to provide an integrated learning experience that will allow the learner (student) partial control over when, where, and how he or she will learn." To illustrate the difference, a model of the flipped classroom should be provided.

A flipped classroom by definition is "a pedagogical model in which the typical lecture and homework elements of a course are reversed. Short video lectures are viewed by students at home before the class session, while in-class time is devoted to exercises, projects, or discussions" (Things You Should Know, 2012).

Here, the definition of flipped classroom cites that it is a form of blended learning. Thus, conceptually, they cannot be the same if one is a subset of the other. Also, the learner does not have a great deal of control over when, where, and how the learning will take place. Typically, the flipped classroom consists of after-school videos, podcasts, or intervention games. The learning has to take place after school. Further, learning outside the classroom via video or podcasts is a necessary step for a successful learning experience in class the next day. In this case the classroom environment is dependent on the outside learning, thus making when and where the outside learning occurs (tonight and at home) mandatory, which no longer allows the student, at least conceptually, control over when and where.

There are some day-to-day functional differences between a flipped classroom and this book's version of blended learning. This book's version of blended learning places the tool as an integral part of learning during the day (in class instruction) as well as outside the school day. This approach to instruction has multiple benefits:

1. The teacher will have an opportunity to model the tool for the students.
2. The teacher will have an opportunity to assess student use of the tool and make corrections when and where appropriate.
3. The teacher will have an opportunity to assess a number of the twenty-first-century skills (such as media literacy) while the student is working, allowing for praise or redirection.
4. The teacher has the ability to allow for intervention, enrichment, and extended learning (when appropriate) experiences outside the school day.
5. Blended learning isn't significantly impacted when students lack devices or Internet at home.
6. Blended learning avoids the "homework trap."

Consider these scenarios:

Teacher A is assigning a flipped classroom assignment that will provide the students an opportunity to view the teacher's lecture (a common flipped classroom practice) on the French Revolution. Also, the teacher assigned a five-minute video to watch on "Storming the Bastille." Students are to enter the classroom the next day armed with the knowledge gained from the flipped assignment.

However, something peculiar occurred overnight. When the students entered the classroom and the teacher began reviewing what should have been covered the previous night, Teacher A realized that 66.6 percent of the students lacked the appropriate background knowledge for the day's activities. It turns out that 33.33 percent of the students did not watch the videos provided and another 33.33 percent did not retain the proper information for the day's activities.

This not only frustrates Teacher A but it also forces Teacher A to cover the content via lecture. Teacher A cannot start the lesson activity until the next day. It turns out to be a two-day lesson.

Teacher B is covering the same topic for his class. As opposed to creating a flipped assignment, he chooses to use blended learning during the next day's class period. When students enter his class, there is an image of a man losing his head. Student are encouraged to go online and answer a question created by the teacher. When the teacher logs on and notices that all student have supplied a response, he then begins to provide direct instruction for five minutes covering the content and linking it to what students have supplied in their responses.

Next Teacher B directs students to a five-minute YouTube video covering the Storming of the Bastille. Each student watches the video on his or her device. Within the video, using the online tool Educanon, Teacher B has inserted two formative assessment questions students must answer to move on with the video. Teacher B is walking the classroom to view student responses and provide clarification and direction when necessary.

Next students are put in pairs but are not told to sit beside each other. The pairs are directed to an interactive timeline and other online sources as well as a Google Doc they must complete. Since students can use Google to collaborate and see their answers in real time, students in pairs do not need to sit beside each other. Again, the teacher walks the classroom to assess students' use of the tool as well as the twenty-first-century skill of collaboration. Again, the teacher can provide clarification and redirection when and where appropriate.

As the class period comes to a close, Teacher B has the ability to look at each student's answers throughout the class. Teacher B realizes that Johnny has missed a number of questions and does not fully understand the content. Teacher B keeps Johnny after class and asks if they could talk about the content after school. Johnny cannot because he has to make sure he and his sister get on the bus.

With this in mind, Teacher B decides to provide Johnny with intervention using the Khan Academy format. Johnny can choose when, where, and how he completes the intervention. The only stipulation is that he must complete it before the upcoming test. Teacher B can also assess the entire class's answers and work. He knows that the students are proficient with the content from the day's class and he plans to move on to an experiential activity the next day. It is a two-day lesson as well.

Reflect on the two scenarios above and consider:

- Which teacher was able to teach students both content and skills?
- Which teacher was able to quickly and accurately assess student comprehension and skills?
- Which teacher, do you feel, is more comfortable with moving on to the experiential learning experience?
- Which teacher, do you feel, left school frustrated? Excited?
- Which classroom experience would you rather have?

WHY BLENDED LEARNING: STUDENTS

Chapter 1 outlined who the twenty-first-century student is and what he or she does. As you recall, the twenty-first-century student is powered up, consumes multiple modes of information, and is constantly connected. Using their devices simply makes sense due to students' everyday use. However, more than that, blended learning has a powerful impact on student achievement. In this section, four recent and highly cited studies will provide clear evidence regarding the impact blended learning can have on student achievement.

- SRI International (Means et al., 2010) used data from more than 1,000 studies ranging from 1996 to 2008. The meta-analysis found that, on average, students in online learning conditions performed modestly better than those receiving face-to-face instruction. The conditions and environment of the students in the study included additional learning time and instructional elements not received by those students in a face-to-face environment.
- The National Education Policy Center conducted a study on Personalized Instruction (Enyedy, 2014). The findings concluded that the best form of technology-integrated education wasn't purely all online and digital. Rather, the strategy of implementing a learning environment that consisted of both face-to-face and digital (blended learning) would reap the largest rewards regarding student achievement.
- RAND researchers in 2013 released a research report. The study focused on the use and results of digital-based software for math tutoring. To accomplish this goal the authors looked at Cognitive Tutor Algebra I created by Carnegie Learning, which is a first-year algebra course that blends classroom instruction and textbook-based activities with computer-based instruction. The RAND assessment used a randomized controlled trial to estimate the effectiveness of the tutoring program in improving algebra proficiency. This two-year study found no results in the first year, but in the second year, students involved in the program increased their performance by eight percentile points. This gain is estimated to be equal to twice the amount of math learned in one full year (Payne et al., 2013).
- In 2014, WestEd published a report focused on digital tools in education, using a game-based learning program in math used in California elementary schools. The report concluded that the program improved students' math scores significantly, when fully implemented. The improvement scores could be seen in the state tests when compared to students who did not participate in the math program (Wendt, Rice, and Nakamoto, 2014).

WHY BLENDED LEARNING: TEACHERS

Certainly, teachers by their nature would make a change simply based on the potential positive impact it could have on students. That is commonplace and common sense. However, as with any change in any organization, it is important for the employee who is directly impacted to know "what's in it for me?" How can a blended learning environment positively impact the teacher?

With the rising demands that are being placed on schools and teachers, coupled with the limited time in the classroom, one of the many solutions to this is a shift to personalized learning and the use of digital devices. This shift can have enormous positive effects on teachers and schools:

- Eager students

  - Motivated
  - Engaged
  - Multiple modes of learning

- Real-time data

  - Assessment data to drive instruction
  - Student friendly data to be used by students for self-regulation
  - Improved feedback to students

- Extended time with students

  - Learn anytime, anywhere

- Collaboration

  - Colleagues
  - Parents
  - Students

- Intervention opportunities

  - Struggling students identified
  - Struggling students receive more focused attention and resources

- Choice for both students and teachers

  - Learning styles can be implemented
  - Instruction that matches student skill

- Prepare students for the twenty-first century and its economy

- When students do better; teachers do better
  - Today's assessment-driven teacher evaluation can be improved with the tools involved in blended learning
- Professional development
  - Any content, anytime, anywhere

Blended learning is a powerful instructional strategy for twenty-first-century students and classrooms. It is important to keep in mind that besides the student, the teacher remains the most important variable in high-quality education. The teacher needs to remain the driver of the educational environment and the device must serve only as a tool. When done appropriately, blended learning can offer big dividends for both the teacher and the students.

3

✦

Skill versus Tools: The Classic Debate of the Chicken and the Egg

The heart of any good educational organization must begin with the question, "What is best for the kids?" The goal of our schools is to prepare our students to be successful in the workplace and to create students who can thrive as employees in the twenty-first-century economy.

If we can prepare students to be successful, then in fact we are doing what is best for the kids. Sadly, however, we are currently not doing what is best for kids. As stated earlier, our schools are not designed to engage or prepare our students to be successful in the twenty-first century.

IF NOT A TWENTY-FIRST-CENTURY DESIGN, THAN WHAT DESIGN ARE WE USING?

The factory design model still permeates the educational environment. To be sure, the factory design was a valid design and did wonders for all institutions—*in the 1800s*! Frederick Taylor, the father of scientific management and the eventual factory system, wanted to solve practical problems that plagued factories all over the country.

He developed the four principles of scientific management. As you read them, note any examples of the use of these principles in our schools:

1. Replace working by "rule of thumb," or simple habit and common sense, and instead use the scientific method to study work and determine the most efficient way to perform specific tasks.
2. Rather than simply assign workers to just any job, match workers to their jobs based on capability and motivation, and train them to work at maximum efficiency.

3. Monitor worker performance, and provide instructions and supervision to ensure that they're using the most efficient ways of working.
4. Allocate the work between managers and workers so that the managers spend their time planning and training, allowing the workers to perform their tasks efficiently (Taylor, 1919).

This new approach to management and organization had a profoundly positive effect. It successfully transitioned the American organization and with it the American economy from chaos to a standardized system of success, the key word being standardized. The economy of the time could be standardized because there was neither organization nor standardization.

The idea of standardization *still rings true* in the hallways of American schools today. It can be seen during class changes, with the ringing of the bell, in the dissemination of information (from the teacher, the expert, to the student), in the organization of management (top-down control starting with the superintendent working its way down to the building principals, the building leadership teams, to teacher leaders to teachers, and maybe all the way down to parents and students), with students entering kindergarten and moving forward one year at a time until they are a completed product, through tracking systems, standardized assessments, and a new standardized curriculum (Common Core State Standards). This is not what our students need.

Our students need a school design that can deliver the needed skills and content for each *individual* to be successful. Individual is the difference between the factory model and the twenty-first-century model. The factory model eliminated individuals and standardized everyone.

Today's students need a curriculum that is individualized to the best of their abilities. For example, students should be able to pass out of second grade if they are ready for fourth-grade academics. Teachers should differentiate instruction to meet the needs of students.

A student in first grade reading at a fifth-grade level should be offered a different reading program than the rest of the class. Students should be provided the option to pursue a career-technical education with the academics embedded in the context of the individual student's specific career interests. A student who is interested in criminal justice should be able to pursue that curriculum. Schools should be able to embed academics in the criminal justice curriculum. For example, during a study of European literature these students should be able to read Sherlock Holmes. In science, criminal justice students should be able to study electricity via Tasers or the ballistics of bullets in physics class.

Students should be given the opportunity to experience real-world problems that are embedded in a curriculum of interest. They should be taught the skill of problem solving. They should be given a curriculum that allows them to solve real-world problems by thinking both creatively and critically.

Students today need a curriculum that engages them to be creative and critical thinkers while being innovative in a collaborative environment. It is ironic that in a time that requires people to be *innovative* to be successful, we seat students in schools that are completely *standardized*!

If I could rewrite Frederick Taylor's scientific management principles for the twenty-first-century schools, they would read:

1. Replace measuring work/success by rote "standardization" and instead use modern social science methods to determine the most efficient way to measure specific tasks.
2. Rather than simply teach all students the same, match student strengths and interests to individual capability and motivation, and teach all of them differently.
3. Assess individual academic and skill performance. Provide instruction and coaching to ensure that all students are using the most efficient ways of learning to achieve self-regulation.
4. Share the work/responsibilities between administration and teachers; teachers and students; remove the functional silo design of education, so that the *team* can spend their time planning, learning, and growing, allowing for greater performance and efficiency from all participants involved.

Partnership for 21st Century Learning (see figure 3.1), a nonprofit, worked with hundreds of businesses and educators to create the skills

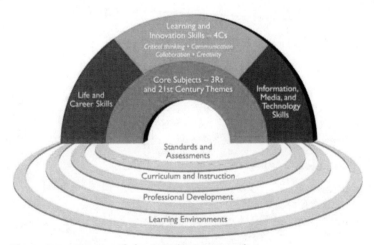

Figure 3.1.   Framework for 21st Century Learning
Partnership for 21st Century Learning, n.d.

that students will need to master to be successful in the twenty-first century. The organization was partly founded with help from OL Time Warner Foundation, Apple Computer, Inc., Cable in the Classroom, Cisco Systems, Inc., Dell Computer Corporation, Microsoft Corporation, National Education Association, and SAP.

The goals of the organization were to create a list of skills students would need. The list consists of the core academic subjects and four twenty-first-century skill themes: (1) 21st Century Interdisciplinary Themes, (2) Learning and Innovation Skills, (3) Information, Media, and Technology, and (4) Life and Career Skills (Partnership for 21st Century Learning, n.d.).

1. Core Subjects:

    a. English
    b. Reading or Language Arts
    c. World Languages
    d. Art
    e. Mathematics
    f. Economics
    g. Science
    h. Geography
    i. History
    j. Government
    k. Civics

2. 21st Century Interdisciplinary Themes:

    a. Global Awareness
    b. Financial, Economic, Business and Entrepreneurial Literacy
    c. Civic Literacy
    d. Health Literacy
    e. Environmental Literacy

3. Learning and Innovation Skills:

    a. Creativity and Innovation
    b. Critical Thinking and Problem Solving
    c. Communication and Collaboration

4. Information, Media and Technology:

    a. Information Literacy
    b. Media Literacy
    c. ICT (Information, Communications and Technology) Literacy

5. Life and Career Skills:

    a. Flexibility and Adaptability
    b. Initiative and Self-Direction
    c. Social and Cross-Cultural skills
    d. Productivity and Accountability
    e. Leadership and Responsibility

This is a powerful list of life and career skills that our students need to obtain. These skills should be purposefully and specifically integrated into daily lesson plans. Teachers should be affluent with the vocabulary of the twenty-first century. It would be to the greater benefit for students to be proficient and well versed in what the skills are. But are they? Are we?

As stated in the introduction, I believe we are not. Part of the reason why is that most educators are enamored with the twenty-first-century tool. And, why not? These tools are fun. Students like them. An engaged student is better than a bored student—even if the student is not learning.

CONTENT IS KING!

The tool is never more important than the learning. Always remember, Content Is King: technology is the tool engaging students within the content. The "what" you are teaching is more important than the "with what."

Surprisingly, failing restaurants can help illustrate this point. In February 2014 Richard Feloni interviewed *Restaurant: Impossible* star Chef Robert Irvine. In this interview he cited five reasons why restaurants fail (Feloni, 2014):

1. Inexperience
2. Bad people management
3. Lack of accounting skills
4. Spotty customer service
5. Subpar food quality and execution

Connecting these five reasons to education, Pam Livingston (2014) explains:

There is no mention of stoves, refrigerators, pots, pans, knives, utensils.
    We need to look at education holistically and not about hardware or software. What is the *experience in the classroom* of the student, what are the factors contributing to that experience, what is the philosophical viewpoint of

that school, what can we change, what can we improve, what do we have to work around, what is the leadership, what do teachers say, what do parents say, what do students say?

Technology can't solve everything, so let's stop simplifying this highly complicated endeavor. All those restaurants which failed within 5 years had stoves, refrigerators, electricity, and gas. That's not the reason they failed. Introducing 1 to 1 without a serious look at everything else can result in pockets of success but not transformation. Take the time, energy and effort to go deeper. (emphasis in original)

Also, remember at the end of the year, teachers and administrators alike are not evaluated on their students' abilities to use multiple digital tools. Rather, teachers are evaluated on the knowledge and skills our students have obtained because they were in our schools and classes. Thus, a rather large emphasis must be placed on both subject matter/content and twenty-first-century skills.

Sure the digital tool is fun, but so are the twenty-first-century skills. Content Is King!

All that being said, it is important to state that our content is fun, too. Referring back to the P21 framework, at the heart of the twenty-first-century skills are the core subjects. Educators attended college and studied specific subjects so they would have the ability to teach them. Therefore, teachers must find these core subjects fun! Further, critical thinking, creating, communicating, and collaborating are what we all do in our daily lives (P21 Learning and Innovation Skills)—and it is fun.

Also, many of us have multiple devices (television, smartphone, tablet, laptop, etc.) that we use to consume media each and every day. We share stories, pictures, and videos with one another. We consume our news media via online stories or video. We upload billions of videos to YouTube. We watch television shows, sports, and movies on these devices. In short, *we are using the Information and Media Skills as outlined by P21 every day*, and it is fun!

Looking at the P21 framework, it seems to scream, "Let's have a party!"

There is no better time to be a teacher. Truly, we have the most exciting and engaging tools to use to teach a twenty-first-century curriculum that is filled with opportunities to learn and have fun. The key is to provide the proper leadership and training to ensure that every teacher fully understands the twenty-first-century skills and has access to the multitude of digital tools.

In the end, it is not the chicken versus the egg conundrum; it is not twenty-first-century tools versus twenty-first-century skills. Rather, it is finding the correct twenty-first-century tool to deliver the twenty-first-century skill/content to the twenty-first-century student!

THE TEACHER MATTERS THE MOST

With all of the wonderful technology that continues to come out at un-precedented breakneck speed coupled with all the state mandates, it is possible to easily forget that the most important resource in every school across the United States, beside the student, is the teacher.

In *What Helps Students Learn* (Wang, Haertel, and Walberg, 1997), the authors researched positive factors on student learning. Two of the most powerful factors illustrate the importance of the teacher. The number 4 and number 14 influencers on student success are teacher–student socialization and student–teacher academic interaction, respectively. Quality of instruction, classroom climate, and classroom instruction scored overall high as well (Wang et al., 1997). Thus the data point to the need for highly qualified and committed teachers—no amount of technology can replace them!

4

✦

Twenty-First-Century Skills and Twenty-First-Century Classrooms

The goal of any education organization is to prepare students to be successful and to successfully participate in the economy. The current economy is different from the economy the average teacher grew up in. The economy of the future will be vastly different from the current economy. This makes educating our students for the future very difficult. How do you prepare students to be successful in an economic environment that is unknown?

That is an excellent question, one that many education and economic philosophers have pondered. However, there is a more pressing question. The greater question is, "How do we educate kids to be successful in the current economy?" As stated earlier, we are preparing students to be successful in Rip Van Winkle's economy.

THEN VERSUS NOW

Many of us had grandparents who were the first among many Americans to drive a car. Much of that was due to Henry Ford. Ford revolutionized the vehicle market with the creation of the assembly line. The assembly line enabled Ford to make more cars at a less expensive cost. Thus, he could sell them at a lower price, allowing most Americans the opportunity to afford a new vehicle. For example, in 1910, Ford could produce one car in twelve hours. For that time in history this was a decent production time for an entire car. However, four years later, in 1914, Ford could produce one car in 1.5 hours (Ford Model T History, 2015)! Between the years

1909 and 1923, Ford was able to cut the cost of one car from $825 to $295 (Late Nineteenth, 2015)! That is advancement.

Of course that advancement doesn't come without a cost. The nineteenth century was known as the century of mass production and industrialization. The scientific management policy (discussed in Chapter 3) made it possible to industrialize and mass produce. Goods could be produced quicker and less expensively, allowing for the masses to be involved in the retail purchase of those goods. One of the many results of the standardization and scientific management approach to business and employee expectations, such as the assembly line, was the nonthinking employees who were a part of an assembly line.

Business was good and the economy boomed. What business and industry needed were employees who must (1) show up on time, (2) show a strong work ethic, and (3) complete a simple task hundreds of times per day. What business and industry did not need were employees who thought for themselves. The jobs of the twentieth century required a very limited cognitive skill—rote memorization.

The schools of the time reflected the needs of the early twentieth-century economy and worker. Schools educated students to at least a sixth-grade level. Schools ensured students had a general foundation in math, reading, and writing. Schools also used the school bell to simulate when the work shift began, when to switch during shifts, when lunch began, and when the day ended. Also, schools mainly engaged students in rote memorization. For purposes of clarifying what schools asked students to do, it is important to define "rote" (Merriam-Webster, 2015):

1. the use of memory usually with little intelligence [learn by rote]
2. mechanical or unthinking routine or repetition [a joyless sense of order, rote, and commercial hustle —L. L. King]

Mechanical and unthinking with little intelligence was the cognitive expectation for the average early twentieth-century student and employee.

The current economy is much different from what early twentieth-century education was designed to produce in our students. Much has changed since the early 1900s. Partnership for 21st Century Learning (Partnership for 21st Century Skills, 2008), the leading think tank focused on twenty-first-century skills, published a report outlining the three drivers for twenty-first-century skills:

1. There have been fundamental changes in the economy, jobs, and business. For most of American history our economy has been based on manufacturing. While that is still a vital part of our economy, it has shifted to a service economy driven by information, knowledge, and innovation.

2. These fundamental changes have also created the need for a new and different skill set. Specifically, in our advanced economy, innovative industries and firms and high-growth jobs require more educated workers with the ability to respond flexibly to complex problems, communicate effectively, manage information, work in teams, and produce new knowledge.

   Postsecondary knowledge will be vital to the sustainability of our economy. This doesn't have to be a four-year degree. This can come in the form of two-year degrees or stackable certificates. In the end, employees of the twenty-first century need to advance their knowledge and have some evidence to prove they possess a specific skill set. Nothing in the twenty-first-century economy suggests that rote cognitive skills will be sufficient!

3. The United States has been focused on closing the achievement gap between the highest and lowest performing students. However, in the same vein, the United States needs to also eliminate the skills gap. That is the gap between the must have skills as identified by U.S. companies and the skills our students are graduating with.

The Programme for International Student Assessment (PISA), an assessment that all developing countries participate in, specifically identifies success on specific measures. Researchers have studied the results of the assessment and their interaction with economic progress. The results are eye-opening.

First, not shocking, cognitive skills are more important than traditional measures of academic success such as grade attainment. It is not how long a student sits in a seat at school but whether or not that child has learned and to what extent while in the seat. It is also important to note that all students, college bound and career bound alike, must possess strong cognitive skills (PISA, 2012). Again, nothing in the twenty-first-century economy suggests that rote cognitive skills will be sufficient!

A second organization, Institute for the Future (IFTF), completed a research report on skills needed in the twenty-first century. The goal of this research was to determine the skills needed by employees in 2020. As did P21, IFTF noted a number of drivers responsible for the change in skills needed for successful employment. Below are their six drivers for change (Institute for the Future, 2011):

- *Extreme Longevity*: Increasing global lifespans change the nature of careers and learning.
- *Rise of Smart Machines and Systems*: Workplace automation nudges human workers out of rote, repetitive tasks.

- *Computational World*: Massive increases in sensors and processing power make the world a programmable system.
- *New Media Ecology*: New communication tools require new media literacies beyond text.
- *Super-Structured Organizations*: Social technologies drive new forms of production and value creation.
- *Globally Connected World*: Increased global interconnectivity puts diversity and adaptability at the center of organizational operations.

Although these are two different organizations researching skills for the twenty-first century at two different times, they do have multiple similarities. Both point to similar driving changes surrounded by technology advancement, data consumption, and mechanical automation. These changes point to a change in skill needed by future employees. Future employees will need to have the ability to process multiple forms of information/data and solicit higher-level cognitive functions utilizing the information. Again, nothing in the twenty-first-century economy suggests that rote cognitive skills will be sufficient!

One dichotomy that compares the purpose of education between the twentieth century and the twenty-first century is that the cognitive challenge of the twentieth century and the twenty-first century is "Rote vs. Rigor and Relevance."

TWENTY-FIRST-CENTURY FRAMEWORKS

In response to the research listed above, P21 created a framework for twenty-first-century skills (see figure 4.1) that today's students need to master to be successful in the twenty-first-century economy.

As you can see in this framework, the twenty-first-century economy will demand both academic and job-embedded skills. Employees of the twenty-first century will need to be able to think both critically and creatively, communicate, and collaborate. They will need to possess technological skills as well as life and career skills, which include (Partnership for 21st Century Skills, 2008):

- Flexibility and Adaptability
- Initiative and Self Direction
- Social and Cross-Cultural Skills
- Productivity and Accountability
- Leadership and Responsibility

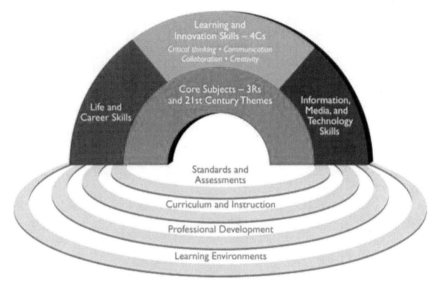

Figure 4.1.   Framework for 21st Century Learning
Partnership for 21st Century Learning, n.d.

It is important to remember that the original policy document identifying the three drivers for twenty-first-century skills was written in
2008. How do these skills, identified by P21 in 2008, still sit and fit with
employers in 2016? Forbes.com staff member Susan Adams writes an an-
nual column outlining what skills employers most want. The results are
derived from a research survey created by the National Association of
College and Employers. The survey asked hiring managers what skills
they plan to prioritize when they recruit from the class of 2014 and 2015
at colleges and graduate schools. Adams reports the following results
(Adams, 2014):

1. Ability to *work in a team* structure
2. Ability to *make decisions* and *solve problems* (tie)
3. Ability to *communicate* verbally with people inside and outside an
   organization
4. Ability to plan, *organize* and prioritize work
5. Ability to obtain and *process information*
6. Ability to *analyze* quantitative data
7. *Technical knowledge* related to the job
8. Proficiency with computer software programs
9. Ability to *create* and/or edit written reports
10. Ability to sell and influence others (emphasis added)

Does this list look as if rote memorization is what twenty-first-century employers are looking for? For the reader's convenience, the 21st Century Skills as laid out by P21, are highlighted in the list above in italics. Adams also reported in 2015 the results shown in table 4.1 (Adams, 2015): where 1 = not essential; 2 = not very essential; 3 = somewhat essential; 4 =essential; 5 = absolutely essential.

Table 4.1.   Essential Work Skills

Skill	Ranking
Critical Thinking	4.7
Teamwork	4.6
Professionalism/Work Ethic	4.5
Oral/Written Communications	4.4
Information Technology Application	3.9
Leadership	3.9
Career Management	3.6

Reviewing the results for both 2014 and 2015, it is safe to state that the framework is still valuable today.

OTHER FRAMEWORKS

In accompaniment to the P21 framework, other organizations have staked a claim as to what twenty-first-century skills should consist of. One such organization that is germane to this topic is Education 20-20.

[Education 20-20] is an international consulting group made up of Carla Cross, Karen Hamilton, Debbie Plested and Mary Rezk. Information Communication Technologies (ICTs) are changing traditional physical communities and creating more global and social networks.

Now and in the future, understanding how to traverse, contribute to, and benefit from these global networks will be a fundamental requirement. A key objective of educational systems should be to foster global citizenship. With these ideals in mind, [Education 20-20] was created to highlight the importance of the fusion of education, citizenship and community. (Education 2020, n.d.)

The ISTE is another organization spearheading the movement to implement twenty-first-century skills in schools to help prepare our students for the twenty-first-century economy. As like the other organizations, ISTE has created their version of a twenty-first-century skills framework. Their framework is shown in figure 4.2 (ISTE, n.d.). As with the P21 skills,

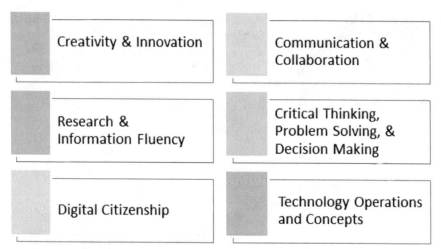

Figure 4.2.   Description: Education 20-20's 21st Century Framework

the need for educators to keep these skills in mind as they plan their instruction and learning experiences for students is paramount.

Another contributing organization to the development of twenty-first-century skills is the Global Digital Citizen Foundation, which implemented what they refer to as the "21st Century Fluencies." Vice president of the foundation and co-author of *Literacy Is Not Enough*, Andrew Churches (2016) outlined the 21st Century Fluencies, which serve as the foundation to their work: Solution Fluency, Creativity Fluency, Collaboration Fluency, Media Fluency, and Information Fluency.

The last organization to research a list of skills needed for the twenty-first century, mentioned earlier in this chapter, is the Institute for the Future (2011), which implemented a comprehensive and methodical process to determine the skills needed for employees in 2020. Their list of skills includes:

- Sense Making
- Social Intelligence
- Novel and Adaptive Thinking
- Cross-Cultural Competency
- Computational Thinking
- New Media Literacy
- Transdisciplinary
- Design Mindset
- Cognitive Load Management
- Virtual Collaboration

A quick scan over all of them will provide the reader with a list that seems compatible to the lists of P21 and ISTE. There are some differences in the skills listed by the organizations above and each organization brings its own bias to the curriculum. Thankfully, these four organizations (and many not highlighted in this book) build upon the thinking of the others, meaning that there are a number of similar skills identified by the differing organizations. A list of those similar skills includes:

1. Problem Solving
2. Critical Thinking
3. Team Work and Collaboration
4. Digital and Media Literacy

These overlapping skills have also been identified as the essential skills for employees by the Economist Intelligence Unit (Driving the Skills Agenda, 2015). These are the key skills that will be further analyzed in the following sections.

TWENTY-FIRST-CENTURY SKILLS DIAGNOSED

A brief orientation of the "shared" twenty-first-century skills is identified below. For purposes of this orientation, this book will address the twenty-first-century skills through the P21 framework due to its dominant standing within the literature. Also, this chapter will not provide a descriptive definition of each of the skills, as that is too broad a concept for one chapter. Thus the reader is urged to research these skills (which can be found at http://www.p21.org/storage/documents/docs/P21_Framework_Definitions_New_Logo_2015.pdf).

Communication and Collaboration

The twenty-first century demands that employees, our future students, be able to articulate their own ideas and thoughts through a number of media forms: oral, written, as well as nonverbal. It is imperative they be able to communicate for more than the singular purpose of passing on information. Rather, students should be able to communicate to instruct others, motivate individuals, and persuade colleagues, customers, or clients to their line of reasoning (P21, 2015).

Students should be able to collaborate with others (both heterogeneous and nonheterogeneous groups). They should be able to work effectively as a team or in diverse groups. Students should assume responsibility for individual and collaborative work; they should value the individual contributions within the team and assert their own meaningful contribution (P21, 2015).

Students should be able to work and collaborate with others. Specifically, they should be able to work creatively by developing, implementing, and communicating new ideas. Students need to be able to listen to diverse perspectives/opinions and be open to different ideas, and they should be able to develop work that is both inventive and original as well as understanding the real-world constraints to inventing. There should be no fear of failure. Failure is a step to learning and success (P21, 2015).

Why This Skill?

It is important that students know all forms of communication from the perception of the person receiving the communication. Therefore, communicating—face to face, texting, or whatever form—requires students to do so in a responsible manner that represents them and the institutions they work for. The workforce of the twenty-first century requires students to interact with individuals around the globe (businesses partner with or house employees in multiple offices encompassing the globe) due to the presence of the Internet. Thus it is essential that our students have the skills needed to collaborate in an effective manner with individuals via both technology and face-to-face settings (Critical 21st Century Skills, 2015).

Critical Thinking and Problem Solving

P21 breaks this section into four subsections: Reason Effectively, Use Systems Thinking, Make Judgments and Decisions, and Solve Problems. Here students need to be able to use both inductive and deductive reasoning when appropriate. Students should be able to understand how the "whole" interacts with various other parts to produce outcomes (P21, 2015).

Students should be able to address problems by effectively diagnosing the problems, identify appropriate evidence, collect the evidence/data, and analyze the evidence/data to create a solution. Students should be able to synthesize information and make relevant connections or link two unrelated pieces of information. They should be able to ask significant questions to clarify a particular point of view which would lead to a potentially better solution (P21, 2015).

Why This Skill?

This skill is important because the problems that we face will only become more complex as time and society move forward. The more opportunities our students have to develop real-world solutions to real-world problems, the more apt they are to be successful (Critical 21st Century Skills, 2015).

Creativity and Innovation

The twenty-first century will ask our students to think creatively. To do so, they must demonstrate the ability to brainstorm or use other idea-curating techniques. They should be able to meaningfully and purposefully create new and worthwhile ideas or concepts. Students should have the ability to evaluate their own ideas and learning. They should be able to elaborate and refine their ideas through careful analysis and evaluation. This is similar to reaching self-actualization in both the classroom and workplace (P21, 2015).

Why This Skill?

Due to the nature of their lives, digital natives, students today are in a constant state of stimulation. They have the ability to both consume and produce information. Students today need to think and work both in the digital and nondigital environment.

Information, Media, and ICT Skills

Information literacy is the ability to access and evaluate information. Students need to be able to access information, evaluate the information, use the information, and manage the information. It is vital that students have the ability to differentiate quality and nonquality information. Also, with the abundant amount of information at our student's fingertips, the ability to manage the flow of information is important. It is imperative that students fully understand and apply both ethical and legal perspective surrounding the access and use of information (P21, 2015).

Media literacy will require students to be able to understand how and why media messages are created and what the purposes for specific media messages are. Media is a powerful medium and it is important that students understand how each medium impacts individual interpretations, values, and points of view, as well as individual beliefs and behaviors. Students need to obtain the skills to use multiple media creation tools. Also, it is imperative students understand and apply both the ethical and legal perspectives surrounding media (P21, 2015).

ICT literacy asks students to apply technology effectively as a tool to research, organize/curate, evaluate, and communicate information. Students need to be comfortable with differing digital devices and technologies (laptops, tablets, smartphones, etc.), communication and network tools, as well as social networks to access, manage, integrate, evaluate, and create information. Also, it is imperative that students understand and apply both ethical and legal perspectives surrounding information technologies (P21, 2015).

Why This Skill?

Tools and technologies are changing at a rapid rate. The ability to have experience in multiple forms of ICT software and tools, stay up to date on these tools, and learn to use new tools is invaluable for today's students.

CONCLUSION

All of the skills outlined by P21, ISTE, IFTF, and the Global Digital Citizen Foundation are certainly worthwhile for students and teachers alike. The skills that our students must possess are vastly different from the ones the average teacher experienced in school or learned in college. Today's economic world looks much different from the economic world of the 1940s. Today's economic world looks much different from that of Rip Van Winkle's day. The rest of the world seems to have moved on in the past one hundred plus years except for schools. Schools have somehow seemed to sputter along.

It is time for a new vehicle. It is time Rip trade in his Model T Ford for something more contemporary, something more fitting for the twenty-first century. It is time for both Rip and schools to trade in their outdated curriculum and adopt the twenty-first-century curriculum, as outlined in this chapter. It is time classroom teachers integrate the new skills and curriculum into their classrooms and engage students in the world in which our students live.

The fear with implementing this new curriculum and new technologies is that schools will forget to ensure that students are thinking. Remember, the tool takes a back seat to the content—content is king! The content must include extensive opportunities for rigorous and challenging thought.

5

✛

Skills Are Important, but Shouldn't Kids Think? Cognitive Models for Student Achievement

Up to this point, this book has pointed to the need for integrating technology and twenty-first-century skills. It is important to note the reasons for higher-order thinking skills and the tools to accomplish this thinking. You will recall from Chapter 4 that many of the twenty-first-century skills require students to analyze, synthesize, and create, among others. These skills certainly are not lower-level thinking skills and do not require rote memorization in the classroom. In fact, it is just the opposite, as this chapter will point out.

WHY INTEGRATE SERIOUS COGNITIVE CHALLENGE AND CONSUMPTION?

In March 2009, President Barack Obama made a bold statement, one that has pushed researchers and educators alike to develop and administer a more cognitively challenging curriculum:

> I am calling on our nation's Governors and state education chiefs to develop standards and assessments that don't simply measure whether students can fill in a bubble on a test, but whether they possess 21st century-skills like problem-solving and critical thinking, entrepreneurship and creativity. (cited in Darling-Hammond & Adamson, 2014, p. 1)

If nothing else, Chapter 4 pointed to the need for our students to experience serious thinking. Gone are the days of rote memorization. Also, teachers cannot get caught up in the flash of the technology and forget about the content. Therefore, the key is to create engaging lesson plans that cover the appropriate content, providing opportunities to engage in twenty-first-century skills, using twenty-first-century tools, while pushing students' "cognitive consumption" forward.

Since then, a new national curriculum, Common Core State Standards, has been written and is in the process of being accepted in a number of states. The curriculum has standards with the goal of teaching and assessing twenty-first-century skills. Also, with the new curriculum comes a new assessment.

There are two consortia creating assessments: the Partnership for Assessment of Readiness for College and Careers (PARCC) and the Smarter Balanced Assessment Consortium (SBAC). As nations around the world begin to develop the new curricula and assessments that are reflective of the twenty-first century, the leaders stand tall in their conviction regarding the need:

> [We need] less dependence on rote learning, repetitive tests and a "one size fits all" type of instruction, and more on engaged learning, discovery through experiences, differentiated teaching, the learning of life-long skills, and the building of character, so that students can . . . develop the attributes, mindsets, character and values for future success. (Ng, 2007)

ASSESSMENT SUCCESS

There have been studies and analysis of the new curriculum. The results of the analysis are enlightening. As the consortia point out, the new curriculum calls for the development of many more complex skills than those that have been typically assessed. In fact, a number of studies illustrate that most standardized assessments measure only recall and recognition (Darling-Hammond and Adamson, 2014). Table 5.1 illustrates the study's findings.

Table 5.1. Percentage of Items at Different Levels of Cognitive Demand on 19 State Tests

	Memorize/ Recognize/ Identify	Implement Procedures	Demonstrate Understanding	Conjecture; Prove/ Analyze	Solve Novel Problems/ Draw Connections
Mathematics	16%	63%	13%	6%	1%
English Language Arts (Reading)	31%	21%	15%	29%	4%

As you can see from table 5.1, the cognitive challenge on the standardized assessments is not great. Between Math and English language arts, only 5 percent of questions asked students to solve novel problems, 48 percent asked students to memorize/recognize/identify, and 84 percent asked students to implement procedures.

Compare these data to predicted assessment questions for the Next Generation Assessments (PARCC and SBAC). The two consortia researching the cognitive demands on the assessments were able to closely analyze the standards for the Common Core curriculum. Based on the cognitive demand of the standards, the consortia predicted the cognitive demand on the assessments. Table 5.2 shows their findings (Herman and Linn, 2013).

Table 5.2. Predicted Assessment Questions Types for the Next Generation Assessments (PARCC and SBAC)

	Overall	Reading	Writing	Speaking/ Listening	Research/ Inquiry
Mean # Content Targets (%)	35 (100%)	14 (40%)	10 (29%)	4 (11%)	7 (20%)
DOK 1	33%	19%	30%	75%	43%
DOK 2	46%	55%	47%	50%	33%
DOK 3	43%	55%	27%	50%	38%
DOK 4	25%	24%	20%	8%	38%

To help clarify, in table 5.2, DOK stands for Depth of Knowledge, derived from Webb's Depth of Knowledge model. This is a cognitive model used to determine cognitive challenge. It is much like Bloom's Taxonomy or Dale's Cone of Learning. DOK 3 and DOK 4 are higher-level cognitive challenging tasks, whereas DOK 1 and DOK 2 are lower-level cognitive challenging tasks.

In short, the Next Generation Assessments, due to the new curriculum and focus on twenty-first-century skills, are much more cognitively demanding. Therefore, it is imperative that we as educators work diligently to prepare our students for this type of assessment. All teachers, K–12, should work on integrating all levels of cognitive demand into their daily lessons and assessments.

ECONOMIC GROWTH

For years education experts and economists have been attempting to connect educational attainment to economic growth. Not only is this clear via research, but it is also common sense; on average, greater educational attainment equals greater labor force participation, higher employment levels, reduced unemployment, and increased earnings (Free Market Competition, 2015). However, as stated earlier, which is also backed up by research, it is not how long a student sits in school that matters, but rather, what matters is what he or she learns.

Not only is education correlated with the economy via standardized assessment, but more specifically, the type of questions students respond correctly to on the standardized assessment also correlates to the economy. A study by Hanushek and Woessmann (2007) "conclude(d), there is strong evidence that the cognitive skills of the population—rather than mere school attainment—are powerfully related to individual earnings, to the distribution of income, and to economic growth."

To further illustrate this point, researchers used forty-five years of Programme for International Student Assessment (PISA) results to determine the connection of cognitive skills, using a valid and reliable assessment, to the economy. The researchers "found that even a small improvement in citizens' academic ability can have a significant impact on the future of a nation's economy, as measured by gains in Gross Domestic Product" (Study.com, 2010).

Interestingly, it isn't just the cognitive skills that correlate to economic prosperity. Researchers have also concluded that "character skills such as personality traits, goals, motivations, and preferences, which are valued in the labor market, in school, and in many other domains" (Heckman and Kautz, 2013) are not accurately captured on standardized assessment such as the PISA. Further the research shows that these "soft skills" do in fact predict success in life (Heckman and Kautz, 2012). These "soft" "noncognitive" skills also influence school decisions, which indirectly also affect wages given those school decisions (Heckman, Stixrud, and Urzua, 2006).

In short, both cognitive abilities and noncognitive abilities (what P21 and other organizations refer to as life skills) are predictors of domestic and individual economic success. Again, the evidence points to the need for teachers to incorporate all levels of cognitive demand in both assessment and lesson planning.

MODELS OF COGNITIVE RIGOR

For a good portion of the early American education system schools and teachers did not have a model guiding them to develop learning experiences with varying levels of rigor. Nor did teachers and schools have a way in which to categorize the various levels of cognitive demand. Therefore, a social scientist, Benjamin Bloom, embarked on this tedious task. While highly intelligent, Bloom wasn't the most creative. When he and his colleagues completed their research, it became widely known as Bloom's Taxonomy.

Bloom and his colleagues originally published their work in 1948. The intent of the original authors was to develop a classification system for educational goals regarding student performance. In 1948, the intent of the research was to focus on three domains of learning: cognitive, affective, and psychomotor. Of their research, the cognitive domain (see table 5.3) has received the most attention. The cognitive domain covered "the recall or recognition of knowledge and the development of intellectual abilities and skills" (Bloom, 1956).

In 1948 the taxonomy contained six categories: knowledge, comprehension, application, analysis, synthesis, and evaluation. Table 5.3 lists the six categories as well as correlating action verbs for each of the categories.

Table 5.3.   Bloom's Taxonomy Verbs

Knowledge	Count, Define, Describe, Draw, Find, Identify, Label, List, Match, Name, Quote, Recall, Recite, Sequence, Tell, Write
Comprehension	Conclude, Demonstrate, Discuss, Explain, Generalize, Identify, Illustrate, Interpret, Paraphrase, Predict, Report, Restate, Review, Summarize, Tell
Application	Apply, Change, Choose, Compute, Dramatize, Interview, Prepare, Produce, Role-play, Select, Show, Transfer, Use
Analysis	Analyze, Characterize, Classify, Compare, Contrast, Debate, Deduce, Diagram, Differentiate, Discriminate, Distinguish, Examine, Outline, Relate, Research, Separate,
Synthesis	Compose, Construct, Create, Design, Develop, Integrate, Invent, Make, Organize, Perform, Plan, Produce, Propose, Rewrite
Evaluation	Appraise, Argue, Assess, Choose, Conclude, Critic, Decide, Evaluate, Judge, Justify, Predict, Prioritize, Prove, Rank, Rate, Select,

Source: http://www.teach-nology.com/worksheets/time_savers/bloom/

Teachers are very aware of this model and use it as part of their daily lesson planning and delivery. But as this book has pointed out, times have changed. Therefore, the traditional teaching methods that have been ingrained into our educational system should undergo a change (when and where appropriate) to meet and match the demands of the current student and economy. Thus in 2005, Bloom's Taxonomy was revised.

In the early 1990s, a student of Bloom, Lorin Anderson, determined that the taxonomy should be looked at closely and consideration should be given to revising it to meet the needs of (then) contemporary education. The new taxonomy viewed thinking as an active process, thus the authors chose to use action verbs for the names of the six individual major cognitive processes: Remembering, Understanding, Applying, Analyzing, Evaluating, and Creating (Krathwhol, 2002). A side-by-side comparison of the two taxonomies, found in figure 5.1, will help to illustrate the differences.

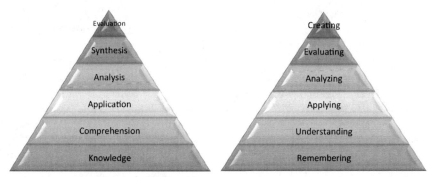

Figure 5.1.   Description: Bloom's original and revised taxonomy.
Criteria for High-Quality Assessment

As can be seen from the two different taxonomies shown in figure 5.1, a significant emphasis has been placed on using verbs to illustrate that thinking is an active process. Within the new taxonomy, evaluating has been moved down a level, synthesis and comprehension have been removed, and creating has been placed at the highest form of cognitive processing.

While Bloom's was the first cognitive taxonomy, it certainly was not the last. Over the years Webb's Depth of Knowledge has gained popularity. This taxonomy of cognitive rigor, developed by Norman Webb from the University of Wisconsin–Madison, was created and published in 1997. The goal of the taxonomy was to develop a framework of differentiating levels or depth of knowledge. In the process of the research, Webb was able to identify four differing depths of knowledge that students should be challenged with. Each of the four groupings reflects a different level of cognitive expectation, or depth of knowledge, required to complete the task (Webb's DOK Guide, 2015). The four levels of cognitive rigor are identified and explained below as well as examples of each.

Level 1: Recall and Reproduction

Tasks at this level require recall of facts or rote application of simple procedures. The task does not require any cognitive effort beyond remembering the right response or formula. Copying, computing, defining, and recognizing are typical level 1 tasks (Aungst, 2014).

Level 2: Skills and Concepts

At this level, a student must make some decisions about his or her approach. Tasks with more than one mental step such as comparing, organizing, summarizing, predicting, and estimating are usually level 2 tasks (Aungst, 2014).

Level 3: Strategic Thinking

At this level of complexity, students must use planning and evidence, and thinking is more abstract. A task with multiple valid responses where students must justify their choices would be level 3 examples, including solving nonroutine problems, designing an experiment, or analyzing characteristics of a genre (Aungst, 2014).

Level 4: Extended Thinking

Level 4 tasks require the most complex cognitive effort. Students synthesize information from multiple sources, often over an extended period of time, or transfer knowledge from one domain to solve problems in another. Designing a survey and interpreting the results, analyzing multiple texts by extract themes, or writing an original myth in an ancient style would all be examples of level 4 tasks (Aungst, 2014).

WHY WEBB'S DOK?

As stated earlier, Webb's DOK is not the first nor is it the only taxonomy of cognitive rigor. So, why use DOK in creating lesson plans or assessments? First, as mentioned earlier in this chapter, many researchers have used the DOK framework as a means for analyzing the cognitive rigor of the new state standards and potential future standardized assessments.

Second, I believe that using Bloom's Taxonomy and the verbs associated with it (see table 5.3) does not necessarily equate to a more rigorous question or deeper understanding. This is because many educators, in practice, actually arbitrarily assign the verbs from a level and believe they are creating more rigorous questions. In reality this is not true because many of the verbs can be found in multiple levels of Bloom's Taxonomy. For example, table 5.4 presents a short list of verbs that can be found in multiple levels. It is just a sampling of the number of verbs that are included in multiple levels of Bloom's Taxonomy. Without a clear understanding of the level and how the verb should be used, many teachers run the risk of unintentionally using the verb alone to determine the level of cognitive rigor.

Table 5.4.   Multiple Levels of Verbs

Verb	Cognitive Level
Describe	Knowledge, Comprehension, Evaluation
Explain	Comprehension, Synthesis, Evaluation
Summarize	Comprehension, Synthesis, Evaluation
Illustrate	Comprehension, Application, Analysis
Predict	Comprehension, Application, Analysis, Evaluation

Third, the belief is that the new standards, the new assessments, and the new expectations of both the state and federal levels of the Department of Education indicate that students simply are not provided with cognitively challenging questions. Rather, the new standards and assessments ask students to master a deeper understanding of content. Webb's DOK does just that. DOK provides a framework for educators to create questions and learning experiences that actively engage students and allow for a greater opportunity for deeper learning and understanding. In fact, Webb suggested that his framework was four ways of describing how a student would interact with the content.

Fourth, and last, it is possible to align all three frameworks (see figure 5.2) discussed thus far, starting with Bloom's original Taxonomy, the Revised Taxonomy, and Webb's DOK.

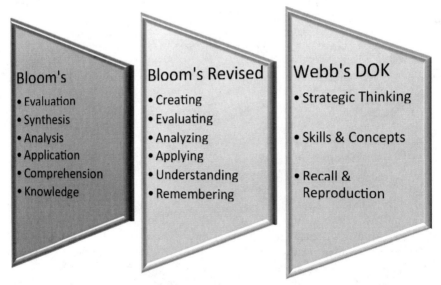

Bloom's
- Evaluation
- Synthesis
- Analysis
- Application
- Comprehension
- Knowledge

Bloom's Revised
- Creating
- Evaluating
- Analyzing
- Applying
- Understanding
- Remembering

Webb's DOK
- Strategic Thinking
- Skills & Concepts
- Recall & Reproduction

Figure 5.2.   Comparison of Bloom's orginal, revised, and WEB's DOK

CONCLUSION

Students today must have the cognitive skills to be successful in the twenty-first-century economy. Simple rote memorization will not do the trick. More specifically, students must have a deeper understanding of the curriculum as well as possess higher-level thinking abilities. The key to creating great learning experiences for the twenty-first-century student that will prepare them for the twenty-first-century economy is integrating twenty-first-century skills, increasing cognitive consumption, while implementing twenty-first-century digital tools.

To this point, this book has covered the twenty-first-century student, twenty-first-century skills, twenty-first-century classroom, as well as cognitive consumption. The rest of this book will propose a model of twenty-first-century learning, a list of twenty-first-century tools, a twenty-first-century lesson plan template, and a district-wide plan for implementation.

6

Stumbling Down
the Right Path

At this point you should have a strong sense of why schools should move to a blended learning environment and be inspired to do so. However, the *how* is another question. This chapter will begin to develop a solution to the *how*. It will address this through a unique process. There really is no one set secret recipe to a successful blended learning initiative. There are, however, a number of school districts that have failed. Within those failures are a number of lessons that all schools should consider.

LOS ANGELES UNIFIED SCHOOL DISTRICT

In 2013, then superintendent John Deasy, with the cooperation of the board of education, approved a one-to-one initiative using Apple iPads in the amount of $400-plus million. The plan was to provide an iPad for each student in the district at $678 per iPad. This would include the iPad, a case, and preloaded educational software. According to Deasy, the rollout was a "civil rights imperative with potential to equalize access to technology" (cited in Iasevoli, 2013).

It didn't take long for major issues or concerns to surface. Due to security issues, more than three hundred students skirted the security on the tablet and surfed social networking sites, so Deasy issued a delay in the rollout. During this delay, other schools, media organizations, researchers, and concerned parents began to ask questions. For example, What is the intended result of the rollout? Why the iPad? Also, a majority of the teachers questioned the continued rollout of iPads as well as stated they did not receive enough training on how to use the device (Iasevoli, 2013).

Fast forward a year. The school district continued to have problems with the initiative. Deasy suspended the district's contract with both Apple and Pearson Publishing. The cost of the initiative is much higher than the original $400-plus million. The total cost of ownership would be over $1 billion. The facilities of the school district were not equipped to handle the digital load of each student carrying an iPad. On top of this, the Federal Bureau of Investigation stepped in to determine how the bidding process went with regard to purchasing the digital tool (Blume, 2015).

At this point, not all students had received an iPad, the training had not positively progressed, and the superintendent and head of technology had both resigned. With respect to Deasy and the Los Angeles Unified School District, many of the issues they faced are not unique to them. Unfortunately, since they are the second largest school district in the nation and this was the largest rollout in educational history, it received a great deal of press.

OTHER BUNGLES AND STUMBLES

Hoboken, New Jersey, school district's closets are filled with laptops lying and getting dusty. Many other laptops are sitting on laptop carts in their last leg. This wasn't always the case. In 2009, when Hoboken adopted the one-to-one initiative, laptops were being used. Unfortunately, they weren't being used for the right reasons. Students would use the Internet to surf sites they were not permitted to visit. School officials placed software on the computers to block students from these sites. Students would still find a way around the filters and would play games online such as Solitaire.

The security software bogged down the laptops, making them slow to start and run. Often the laptops would crash shortly after starting. Therefore, many students could not use the laptop in the classroom. Students were bringing laptops to be fixed on a daily basis, which overworked an already overworked staff.

Teachers at Hoboken complained of too little training on how to use the device in the classroom. The device, said the teachers, distracted students from learning. This is a symptom of not knowing how to manage a classroom with devices. Most of the community knew the Wi-Fi password and would unintentionally jam the network by logging on. The system became unusable and the devices were unsustainable (Barshay, 2014).

Similarly, a large school district, Fort Bend, Texas, faced many issues when rolling out the one-to-one initiative. The school district of 70,000 students offered every student, from second to eighth grade, iPads (total-ing 63,000 devices). After nineteen months the district halted its plan and rollout. The reasons were unrealistic goals (an overly aggressive timeline), insufficient planning, short-sighted and poor project management, and the digital courses did not match the standards being taught (Ravitell, 2013).

MISTAKES MADE = LESSONS LEARNED = ROAD MAP

According to Michigan's One to One Institute (2015), over 2,000 schools are operating some form of a one-to-one initiative. The National Survey on Mobile Learning found that 71 percent of schools surveyed have adopted some form of mobile technology in the classroom. Eighty-one percent of the districts were considering a one-to-one implementation in the next two years (Steckner, 2015). The levels of intensity vary from school to school but many of the problems faced during this rollout are the same:

- Lack of professional development,
- Inability to connect device to instruction,
- Too many learning initiatives and teachers are bogged down in the bureaucracy of school reform,
- Lack of contract management skills,
- Lack of safeguards to protect the device and student data,
- Lack of a clear vision for the rollout,
- Lack of a clear plan to sustain the rollout,
- Not clearly understanding the total cost of ownership (TCO),
- A focus on student consuming information as opposed to meaning-ful and purposeful creation,
- Lack of buy-in from teachers and especially teacher leaders,
- Setting unrealistic timelines and goals,
- Lack of manpower in the tech department to handle the devices,
- Lack of patience and time for the rollout to be successful (it is a mara-thon not a sprint),
- Lack of parental involvement (4 Lessons from K–12 Ed Tech Failures, 2014; Hooker, 2015; Steckner, 2015; Wlodarz, 2013).

That is a large list of mistakes and to be sure there are more than that. Also, none of these are isolated mistakes by one school. Not all of the mis-takes listed above are made by all schools. The list of common mistakes and stumbling blocks can be narrowed down. A meta-analysis of these reported stumbling blocks will provide a list of common issues that a high percentage of all schools face. This list includes:

- Professional development

  - Sadly, many schools do not have a full view of the preparation needed to successfully rollout a one-to-one initiative. It has always held true that for schools to be successful their students and teachers must first be successful. This is still the case for a one-to-one environment. The device is not the be-all and end-all. The device does not do the teaching. The teacher is still the main facilitator of education in the classroom.

    Unfortunately, many of our teachers have not received the proper training in their college education for blended teaching. Therefore, it is imperative that schools take the lead. Schools must provide high-quality professional development for their staff members.

  - For many schools across this nation, high-quality professional development is rare. Schools typically provide professional development through a cookie-cutter approach; a one size fits all design of professional development. With technology this approach is woeful in its ability to provide teachers the proper training. Still, many schools use the "if you provide it, they will learn" or the "if you drop the device into the classroom, put it into the hands of the teacher, magic will happen" approach. This just simply is not the case. This approach does not work.

  - When schools do provide professional development, quite often it is centered on functionality of the device. While that is certainly important, once the teacher has mastered the functionality of the device, it is imperative to provide the teachers with professional development that focuses on using the device as an instructional tool, again, something that is woefully missing from many of our schools professional development plans.

- Contract management, security, and student data and security

  - Many schools fall prey to not fully understanding and comprehending the minute details of the contracts they have set up with vendors. For instance, what will the vendor do with the data they compile or have access to, especially regarding student privacy data?

- Sustainability

  - Schools have learned that it can be easier to purchase the device, due to current money streams or grants. However, what happens when the grant runs out, the money stream changes, or device and software costs change? Is the one-to-one movement sustainable in the face of many unknown scenarios?

- Total cost of ownership (TCO)

  - Schools fall prey to not fully seeing the total cost to own the device. The initial purchase price is negotiated and made public, but the hidden costs of total ownership can sneak up on schools. What is the cost of repairing devices? How many tech people will be needed to ensure that all students have a usable device each and every day? Have schools factored in the cost of replacements? Are the infrastructure, Wi-Fi, and servers able to handle the traffic? Will there be any additional costs in the future for updated software or updated contracted services through third-party vendors?

- Lack of a vision and buy-in

  - A common mistake of schools has been a top-down approach to the adoption and rollout of the one-to-one initiative. Have teachers been involved in the process? Do teachers have a say in which device is purchased? Do teachers feel as if they are prepared to teach in a blended environment? Do students feel as if they can be successful in a blended environment? This is a paradigm shift in how school has been done, and it is imperative that leaders address this change with the support, involvement, and blessings of all the stakeholders.

- Unrealistic timeline and goals

  - Unrealistic timelines and goals can hurt a school district. Some schools have rushed the process of deciding what device to purchase to make an implementation deadline. Some schools have not fully prepared their staff in order to meet a timeline. Some schools have fallen short of student achievement goals because they either believed the device itself would enhance the educational experience and thus student achievement or teachers were not fully trained on how to use the device effectively for classroom instruction. It is important for schools to remember that a successful one-to-one initiative is not a sprint but rather a marathon.

- Choose the proper device: functionality versus fad

  - Schools get caught up in the hype of the device as opposed to what the students need. Apple makes a great product and it has revolutionized education. But an iPad cannot run the software that is needed for computer-aided design (CAD) programs. Many tablets today have a layer of convenience because they are touch-screen. However, quite often the keyboard is a part of the screen. Students have shown they are not successful with using those keyboards.

Schools must have an understanding of the needs of the students, teachers, and the programs. Once schools develop their needs, then they should choose a device that best fits those needs.

The scope of this book is not wide enough to look at each of the items listed above in detail. Rather, this book's goal is to dive deep into what teachers can do in their classroom and what school leaders can do and provide for these teachers. Therefore, the rest of this book will focus on providing a solution to the common mistake of a lack of quality professional development. The focus will be on training teachers how to use the tools for instructional purposes in the classroom as well as integrating twenty-first-century skills and cognitive consumption into lesson planning.

7

✝

ART: A Three-Step Process to Blended Learning

Chapter 6 was a summary of the many mistakes that schools districts have made in implementing a successful one-to-one educational initiative. While no educational reform is perfect, schools would do well to try to minimize the number of stumbling blocks they encounter during such an initiative. As stated earlier, the scope of this book is not wide enough to tackle all of the common stumbling blocks listed in previous chapters. However, it is certainly possible to provide schools with an essential piece to a successful one-to-one initiative, that is, guidance on how to use the device properly in the classroom.

This chapter will introduce a technology integration model that is both commonsensical and innovative—the Martin ART model. While the Martin ART model is not much different from other technology integration models, it does offer schools an innovative approach to teaching the model, identifying the individual teacher's skill level within the model, as well as an easy-to-understand skill ascension process.

TEACHING IS AN ART

Teaching is not easy. Regardless of the hype that business professionals or political elitists espouse on glorified news programs, teaching is not easy. There is a great deal of science that accompanies good teaching—some of it has been written about in this book. The science of learning is a truly remarkable field and one that holds much promise for educators. That being said, as much as teaching is a science, it is more so an art.

Consider an artist. Artists learn the science behind different paints, different brush strokes, and different canvasses. The science can certainly inform and help the artist, but it is not the art. The artist still has to have a visual of what the painting or picture should look like. The artist still has to ensure that the piece of art will convey a certain emotion to its viewers. Science can drive art but it isn't the art.

Teaching is much the same. The science of how students learn, the science of data analysis, the science of "wait time," or the science of natural lighting (to name a few) are all very helpful to teaching, but they are not teaching. The science can inform the teacher but it is not teaching. The act of building relationships, reading body language, using empathy, engaging students with personality, or incorporating all that we know about learning into a well-designed lesson that is differentiated for multiple uniquely different learners is teaching. Actually, teaching is much more than that!

Teaching is an art. It is important that all teachers know this. Therefore, teaching with technology is also an art. Due to this knowledge, it is important that the word *art* be a part of the integration model of blended learning.

For many years, schools have participated in a process called "best practices." This book follows the model that a "best practice" is methodically sound research outlining education interventions that are proven to be successful in a specific context. When there is a great deal of data supporting the success of certain practices, it behooves educators to share and adopt them. This is a form of evidence-based education, which is using professional experience and knowledge from quality research as well as classroom data when making instructional decisions.

For the past two decades researchers have been hard at work developing best practices and models for technology integration. This is an overwhelming task for a number of reasons. First, there are so many teachers in the nation and so few researchers interested in the topic. Second, technology integration doesn't really have a common definition. For some teachers PowerPoint is technology integration, for others, it is a Smart board, and still for some it is BYOD (bring your own device). This has made it difficult to standardize, in a conceptual model, technology integration. Third, because technology is changing at such breakneck speed it is difficult to keep up with how it is being used.

In the past twenty years there have been some very relevant and useful models of technology integration: Clayton Christensen Institute, TPACK, SAMR, and RAT. After a brief description of these published models, this chapter will introduce the author's model, known as ART, what the acronym stands for, the diagnostic power of the model, and a lesson integration example.

CLAYTON CHRISTENSEN INSTITUTE

The Clayton Christensen Institute (Christensen Institute, 2015) is a non-profit, nonpartisan think tank devoted to improving areas of our life, such as education, through disruptive innovation (such as digital devices). The institute through years of research was able to define and describe four models of blended learning. The four models are shown in figure 7.1.

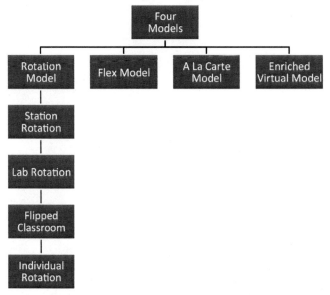

Figure 7.1.   Description: Clayton Institutes model for Blended Learning

Blended Learning Definitions. (n.d.). Retrieved November 14, 2015, from Clayton
   Christenson Institute for Disruptive Innovation, Website: http://www.christen
   seninstituue.org/bleded-learning-definitions-andmodels/

Figure 7.1 defines the institutes' definition of blended learning, which is a combination of brick-and-mortar with online learning. The graphic also displays the four models: Rotation Model, Flex Model, A La Carte Model, and Enriched Virtual Model. You will also notice the Rotation Model has four submodels: Station Rotation, Lab Rotation, Flipped Classroom, and Individual Rotation (Clayton Christensen Institute, 2015). A short explanation of each follows.

1. Rotation Model: a course or subject in which students rotate on a fixed schedule or at the teacher's discretion between learning modalities, at least one of which is online learning.
2. Flex Model: a course or subject in which online learning is the backbone of student learning, even if it directs students to offline activities at times. Students move on an individually customized, fluid schedule among learning modalities. The teacher of record is onsite, and students learn mostly on the brick-and-mortar campus, except for any homework assignments. The teacher of record or other adults provide face-to-face support on a flexible and adaptive as-needed basis through activities such as small group instruction, group projects, and individual tutoring.
3. A La Carte Model: a course that a student takes entirely online to accompany the seated course. The teacher of record for the A La Carte course is the online teacher. This differs from full-time online learning because it is not a whole-school experience. Students take some courses A La Carte and others face-to-face at a brick-and-mortar campus.
4. Enriched Virtual Model: a course or subject in which students have required face-to-face learning sessions with their teacher of record and then are free to complete their remaining coursework remote from the face-to-face teacher. Online learning is the backbone of student learning when the students are located remotely. The same person generally serves as both the online and face-to-face teacher (Clayton Christensen Institute, 2015).

TPACK

TPACK, which stands for Technological, Pedagogical, and Content Knowledge, was created by Mathew Koehler (2011). It was designed to identify the knowledge that teachers needed to teach in a digital environment. The core of the framework (as shown in figure 7.2) is the interplay between knowledge of technology, pedagogy, and content. These three concepts do not work in isolation. Rather, they work together to create a digital learning experience.

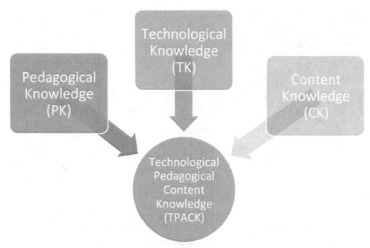

Figure 7.2. Description: TPACK Model
http://www.matt-koehler.com/tpack/tpack-explained/

SAMR

The SAMR model, created by Dr. Ruben Puentedura, was implemented to help identify how technology is being used in the classroom and how it may impact teaching and learning. The model identifies four levels of technology use in the classroom (see figure 7.3): Substitution, Augmentation, Modification, and Redefinition (Technology Is Learning, n.d.).

Figure 7.3. Description: SAMR Model
Image the creation of Dr. Ruben Puentedura, Ph. D.; http://www.hippasus.com/rrpweblogTechnology is Learning, NA

RAT

Produced by Dr. Joan Hughes (Hughes, Thomas, & Scharber, 2006), RAT, is an acronym for Replace, Amplify, and Transform. Hughes proposes a clear framework to assess technological use in the classroom (see figure 7.4). To her credit, I believe the RAT framework is clearer in articulating the three steps than the other frameworks mentioned.

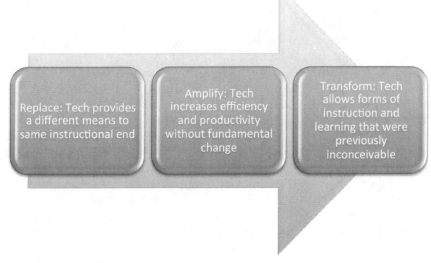

Figure 7.4.   Description: RAT Model
Hughes, Thomas, Scharber, 2006

What each of these models lacks is any explanation of what digital tool to use, suggestions on how to use the digital tool, an explanation of how to integrate technology into a lesson plan, a lesson plan template, as well as any specific use of cognitive or twenty-first-century skills. While these models certainly are useful to describe categories in which technology is used, they really do not present a usable resource for tech-challenged or tech-savvy educators.

NATURAL/ORGANIC

It seems very probable that there are a number of similarities found in the models mentioned above, especially the SAMR and RAT models. There is a very important reason for the similarities between the two, which I will cover shortly. First, it is important to highlight the similarities, as shown in table 7.1.

Table 7.1.   Similarities of the SAMR and RAT Models

SAMR Model	RAT Model
Substitute	Replace
Augment/Modify	Amplify
Redefinition	Transform

Teachers throughout the nation have been implementing and integrating technology into the classroom and for the most part without researched best practices. The use of technology has been both varied and widespread. And yet multiple researchers were able to identify multiple models of similarity regarding technology integration.

This is, in part, because the way technology has been implemented or integrated has been innately human. In other words, integration has flowed from educators in a natural and organically human process. It is a part of the DNA, so to speak, of both teachers and schools.

To help illustrate this point, a story from Biz Stone's new book (Stone, 2015) will be helpful. Biz Stone, cofounder of Twitter, tells a story regarding the use of technology, namely Twitter, and how it has been adapted and utilized by its users. The story is about the University of California at Berkeley. When UC of Berkeley was being built, the project management team chose to complete the buildings and then add the grass. Once the buildings and grass were completed, the builders left. They waited until after the first year of school had come to an end and then they came back, with the purpose of putting in sidewalks and walkways. When the builders came back, they simply looked at the paths the students had made and laid out their sidewalks. The builders were smart enough to know that they could not determine what would be the best path for students to take from building to building. So, instead, they allowed the users to create an emergent path, one that was organic to the students.

It is ignorant to believe that one individual can come up with the perfect way for everyone to utilize technology in education. Rather, it is better for a group of individuals to observe how educators have naturally used technology in the classroom. The individual is rarely smarter than the collective. Chance really does favor the connected educator.

Whether the ART process is right or wrong, in the absence of researched best practices, is neither here nor there. What is important to understand is this is how teachers have naturally come to operate. As stated earlier, it is part of their DNA.

This book takes the stance "Why fight what is innately human and a part of educators' DNA? Instead, embrace it!" In the absence of researched best practices, educators should focus on what is innate and natural. This book develops a theory of technology integration with this in mind. Based on the similar results of different researchers and different models, this book offers a model that is based on these similarities.

THE ART MODEL

Having researched and read about these models coupled with personal experiences, this book provides a model of technology integration, the

Table 7.2.   The Evolution of the ART Model

SAMR	RAT	ART
Substitution	Replace	Assimilate
Augment/Modify	Amplify	Redesign
Redefinition	Transform	Transfigure

Martin ART model, which stands for Assimilate, Redesign, and Transfigure. The evolution of the ART model is shown in table 7.2.

Before each of the steps of the ART model is explained, it is important to note the power of the diagnostic process behind the ART model.

Good teachers know that when they are teaching new students or new content they need to diagnose what the students know both individually and collectively as a class. Therefore, good teaching begins with a diagnostic assessment to determine this information. The results of the diagnostic assessment benefit both the teacher and the student. They know where the students are and where they need to be by the end of the grading period or year. For example, if Teacher A assessed his student's knowledge of the French Revolution via a pretest, would it be helpful to know that Johnny scored a 35?

$$Johnny \ X \ Pretest \ score = 35$$

The answer should be no. There is an important piece of information missing. Johnny's score of 35 is relative to what? In this case the score of 35 is relative to 100. Now, is this information helpful?

$$Johnny \ X \ Pretest \ Score = 35/100$$

Certainly, most people would agree that this bit of information carries more value, with 0 being the lowest Johnny could score and 100 being the highest. Both the teacher and Johnny know that he has a lot of work to do to get to 100!

The illustration is important because it points out the need for a standardized relative continuum (see figure 7.5).

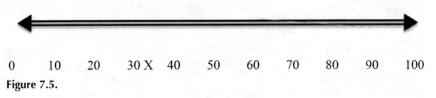

0   10   20   30 X   40   50   60   70   80   90   100

Figure 7.5.

Placing a bold X on the number line at 35 becomes meaningful for both Johnny and the teacher. It shows Johnny and his teacher where he is in regard to mastering the content knowledge and how far he needs to go. Do we have such a standardized relative continuum for technology integration? If it exists, it is very difficult to find. Therefore, this book suggests just such a model, and I have called it the ART model.

Relating to the analogy above with Johnny, would it be beneficial to know the technology integration knowledge and skill of both the individual teacher and your teaching staff as a collective? Sure it would. Since it is beneficial to know this, let's assume leaders used the Martin ART model diagnostic assessment and discover a teacher, Janny A, scored at the Assimilate level. Would this knowledge be beneficial?

Janny A = Assimilate

Not necessarily. Sure, we have more information now than we did before, but the knowledge is relative to what? Is Assimilate a good score? If not, what is a good score?

Again, as in the previous analogy, it would be most helpful if schools had a relative standardized continuum for which to compare the diagnostic score. Figure 7.6 presents the ART continuum.

For this scenario, based on the ART diagnostic assessment, Janny A's score falls in the Assimilate category. With this new information before

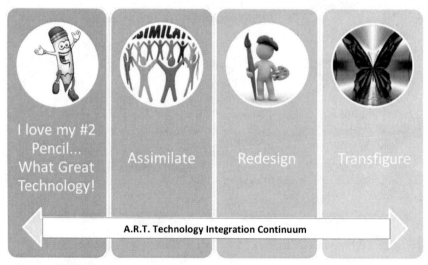

Figure 7.6.   Description: ART Model
Dr. Martin; Abstract Red Butterfly by 7 Themes.com; Happy Pencil created by Jonata 2010-12-13; Assimilate created by First Baptist Church of Rogersville 2015-01-20

you, the continuum, is this diagnostic information more helpful? The answer is yes. The school leader and the teacher both know where the teacher falls on the continuum and both have an idea of what this teacher needs to do to advance.

THE ART MODEL DEFINED

Now that the purpose of having a relative continuum is clear, it is important to explain the three stages of the continuum. Below is a brief explanation of each stage (Assimilate, Redesign, and Transfigure), however, there will be no digital tools or lesson plan templates presented here; those will be presented in Chapter 8.

Assimilate

Assimilate is defined as "cause (something) to resemble; liken" (Google definition).

Technology for many teachers is an overwhelming concept. It is much different from anything they know or want to know. It changes so quickly that the very thought of incorporating technology is daunting. These teachers have had so much bad luck or poor results with using technology that they have no faith in their abilities or the ability of the technology to impact student achievement.

Therefore, it is important to start providing training that will be both basic and beneficial. This is the first step of integration—Assimilate. This step is designed to take what basic tasks teachers are currently doing without technology and *assimilate* the task into the blended environment. These are tasks that are *actionable* and would easily *acclimate* the teacher to the technology and the concept of integration.

Redesign

Redesign is defined as "design (something) again in a different way" (Google definition).

In this stage of technology integration, the teacher is beyond basic assimilation and has worked to improve his or her technology integration into the classroom and instruction. As opposed to simply using technology to replicate what the teacher did in class for decades, the teacher will *redesign* the lesson plan and focus on *ramping* up the use of technology to *reconstruct* how learning is accomplished.

Transfigure

Transfigure is defined as "transform into something more beautiful or elevated" (Google Definition).

At this stage educators are accustomed to using technology in the classroom and reconstructing learning experiences to engage the twenty-first-century student. At this point the teachers' use of technology is no longer to assimilate or redesign learning experiences, but rather, the educator looks to create a learning experience that could not previously have been accomplished.

In essence, the technology has allowed for specific learning experiences that were neither possible nor conceivable before. At this point the teacher has *transfigured* the lesson by *toppling* the primordial walls of the classroom and *tech-necting* students and the learning experience outside the classroom (tech-necting = using technology to connect students through innovative learning experiences/practices to opportunities, people, and areas of the world they would otherwise not experience).

ART Example

To help illustrate the Martin ART model and how it looks, figure 7.7 briefly outlines the use of technology in each of the ART steps. For purposes of this example, a government lesson will be used. The focus of this government lesson is to identify party platforms and political planks of presidential primary candidates.

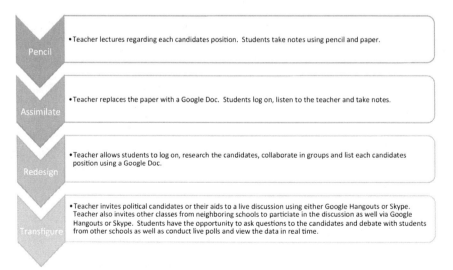

Figure 7.7.   Description: ART Model Example

Figure 7.7 provides an example of the different levels of technology used in each stage of the Martin ART model and how it may be used. As you can see, there is a certain degree of skill, knowledge, and sophistication the teacher must possess as he or she moves through the model. In the beginning simple paper and pencil is the technology, next it is a rudimentary use of Google to assimilate lessons, then the power of Google and online resources is used to redesign opportunities for research and collaboration, and finally the learning experience is transfigured, allowing students to learn the content firsthand through the candidates themselves or trusted aids while having the opportunity to ask questions and debate with candidates and other students.

8

✛

The Three-Stage Process to the ART Model of Blended Learning

This chapter will provide a short summary of each of the three stages of the ART model. It will then provide a series of digital tools, coupled with a summary of the tool and the tools features, which could be integrated into a lesson plan focused on that particular stage of the ART model. Also, at the end of each stage, a lesson plan example is included for teachers. The lesson plan will incorporate twenty-first-century skills and cognitive consumption, as well as digital tools (everything this book has covered to this point).

The hope is that teachers, administrators, curriculum coaches, and other school personnel are able to learn what multiple digital tools can do, how to incorporate both twenty-first-century skills and cognitive consumption into a lesson plan, and how each of the three stages differ from one another. However, it is important to also illustrate that the Transformation level isn't the panacea of education. Good technologically integrated classroom instruction will incorporate all stages of the ART model at different times of the school year. Using expensive technology too much at the Assimilate stage is not a good use of tax dollars. It would be wise for schools to use the robust powers of the technology and digital tools beyond the Assimilate stage as much as possible.

Also, it is important to note that these digital tools are not solely relegated to the stage they have been classified in. It is possible to use a digital tool at varying stages of the ART model. The book has the tools classified into a specific stage because it is believed, based on the features, that it *best* fits in that stage. Teachers, once they are comfortable with the stages, should feel free to use the digital tools listed in any stage he or she feels would maximize a learning situation.

Lastly, when developing the list of tools which will follow, special attention was given to free tools. While some may have a cost, usually it is low and the features of the tool far outweigh the cost. Tools with a cost will be marked by ($$) dollar signs.

ASSIMILATE

This stage in the ART model is focused on helping teachers to bridge the gap from no technology integration to a little integration. Thus, the goal is to make this stage as achievable and easy as possible. In this stage the goal is for the educator to use a few digital tools that are user-friendly to assimilate some standard classroom practices.

An Assimilation stage integration would consist of the teacher using a digital tool to assimilate the same process and product as the pen/pencil and paper method would have. Also, it is important to remember that the Assimilation stage would have the teacher use a digital tool on a task that would be immediately actionable and would begin to acclimate the teacher into the technology.

For example, Teacher X, in the second-grade classroom, typically provides a workbook for spelling words. The students look at the week's spelling words and write a sentence using the word properly as well as spelling it properly. Assimilation integration could have Teacher X share the words with students via Google Docs. The students could then write a sentence using the word properly on the Google Doc. The student can save the assignment in a folder for Teacher X to grade from anywhere he or she has an Internet connection.

Below is a list of digital tools that teachers can use at the Assimilation stage of the ART model.

Assimilation Digital Tools

Comic Puppets Lite

ComicPuppets for the iPhone, iPad, and Android provides a number of tools for students to be creative. Students can use the gallery of characters and backgrounds or create new images with photos. Students decide the position of the character and use the joint and limb features to create the illusion of movement. Students can add wigs, hats, expressions, and objects. They can also fill the balloons with humor, data, historical interpretation, etc. (Comic Puppets Lite, 2015).

Comic & Meme Creator

This app allows educators and students to create Comics, Memes, Bitstrips and Funny pictures. Students can share them with friends on Facebook, Twitter, and by e-mail. They can create Marvel style or Dilbert style comics or funny pictures with a camera. The app includes super heroes and villains such as Spiderman, Captain America, Hulk, Batman, etc. It also includes cartoon characters like the Simpsons, Mickey Mouse, Bugs Bunny etc. as well as a host of custom characters and objects (Comic & Meme Creator, 2014).

The features of the app are: More than 100 popular images for creating memes, 50+ characters, over fifty objects and over fifty backgrounds for use in comics, add Photos from Camera or Gallery and use them in your Comics, ability to preview a comic, save comic/meme as image in gallery, share on Facebook, Twitter, e-mails, and more (Comic & Meme Creator, 2014).

History in Pictures (Android app)

History in Pictures is an interactive guide to the latest pictures of historical events from around the world. The easy-to-use interface and photos bring history to life. App features include: hundreds of historical photos including people, wars, events, and creative moments from world history, view only the pictures which have been shared in the past twenty-four hours, change background themes from light to dark, tap images to see a higher quality and zoom-in on the picture, and share the photos you find with friends via Facebook, Twitter and e-mail (History in Pictures, 2014).

Learn World History (Android app)

Learn World History is a historical dictionary as it contains 2,360 plus entities about world history. Learn World History is an easy and simple to use history app. "No need to Google any names, events and dates or turn hundreds of pages to obtain the desired solution. Everything you need to know about world history is on the palm of your hand.

"Learn World History gives you an opportunity to test your learning with its series of history quizzes. Learn World History provides its user with various categories which makes using this history dictionary, a child's play" (Learn World History, 2015).

The app features are: "Today In History—a feature that tells you what happened in history in today's date, Glyph Translator—users can change your name into ancient history glyph, Quiz—race against time guessing the answers with history quiz, Staples—you can save what you have learnt to revise later in this history dictionary, Contribute—If you have something we don't, contribute it in this history dictionary and we will showcase your it" (Learn World History, 2015).

United States Constitution (Android app)

This app "is easy to navigate, has a real table of contents broken down by articles, sections and amendments, is searchable, and contains other related documents, ideas, and trivia like the Declaration of Independence, Gettysburg Address, The Virginia Plan, The Great Compromise, ratification dates, and many others" (United States Constitution, 2012).

"Features of the app are: searchable US Constitution and Articles of Confederation, resizable text, ratification Dates of Amendments, bios of the signers, Constitution timeline, Declaration of Independence, Articles of Confederation, Gettysburg address, Mayflower Compact, Declaration of the Rights of Man and of the Citizen, Star-Spangled Banner, Emancipation Proclamation and many others" (United States Constitution, 2012).

Smithsonian Channel (Android app)

"Keep up with Smithsonian Channel's original series and documentaries, and explore our vast video library with the NEW Android app. This app introduces a brand new way to watch, find, and explore over 1,000 short videos and free full episodes" (Smithsonian Channel, 2015).

Features include: "vibrant and intuitive design to enhance user experience, thousands of free videos, rotating selection of free full episodes, Quick Picks section that individually selects videos for you based on your interests, new curated playlists, smart auto-play mode to continuously play related videos, Chromecast integration, ability to favorite videos, Facebook, Twitter, and email sharing capabilities, artifacts quiz section where you can put your knowledge to the test, and Channel Finder to check on-air availability" (Smithsonian Channel, 2015).

Discovery Channel (Android app)

"Users can watch thousands of clips and selected full episodes from Discovery Channel shows like Deadliest Catch, Gold Rush, MythBusters, and more! Watch full Discovery Channel episodes, straight from the app! Check out custom-curated playlists, watch the hottest clips from all of Discovery's shows, and share your favorites with friends on Facebook, Twitter and email!" (Discovery Channel, 2013).

World Map Atlas (Android app)

Students have the ability to view a large quick reference world map on an Android device. The app contains Up-To-Date World Maps. Features of the app include: "Political World Map Atlas, find a country easily with a convenient globe map, educational reference map for students, school, and university, up to date maps, view every nation and its major cities in one large map, no internet connection is required. A quick reference map to quickly find countries and cities" (World Map 2015, 2015).

Davinci Note (iPad app)

Davinci note lets teachers or students create and share beautiful notes easily. Make your next note better with Davinci Note's design, image layout, and editing options. Creative students will "appreciate how Davinci Note contains all the essential features and nothing that gets in your way. Capture your thoughts, send messages, and share on blogs in distinctive style" (iTunes Preview, 2013).

QuotesCover

"QuotesCover.com turns any ordinary quotes texts into beautiful quotes picture for Facebook, Twitter header, Google Plus, E-Cards, Wallpapers, Pinterest, Posters and other print design." This app allows students to make a message or saying more memorable by making it more "eye-catchy." However, designing is a complex process that involves things like typography, shapes, color combination, composition, and so forth. Students do not need to think of all of that. "Let QuotesCover application handle the process and you just choose the results" (QuotesCover, 2015).

Visme (presentation tool)

This allows students to tell better stories as well as give them the ability to visualize their ideas into engaging presentations and infographics (Visme, 2015).

PBS Learning Media

PBS offers a number of videos and other interactive resources which are available for students on their website that look at math in different contexts, for example, Math Magic and Money Math. The site lists the grade level for which each resource is appropriate (PBS, 2015).

Multiplication.com

"Multiplication.com provides a mix of free and paid material to teach kids about math. Included in the free resources are a Fact Navigator that helps students learn their multiplication tables, quizzes, and a large number of games" (Hicks, 2015).

MathDudePodcast

"The Math Dude makes understanding math easier and more fun than your teachers ever led you to believe was possible. Host Jason Marshall provides clear explanations of math terms and principles, and his simple tricks for solving basic algebra problems will have even the most math-phobic person looking forward to working out whatever math problem comes their way" (Marshall, 2015).

Padlet ($$)

"Padlet is the easiest way to create and collaborate in the world. It works like a sheet of paper where you can put anything (images, videos, documents, text) anywhere, from any device (pcs, tablets, phones), together with anyone" (Padlet, 2015).

"Padlet makes it easy for teachers to upload questions and pictures as prompts for students. Due to its accessibility from any device teachers are adapting it to gauge student learning through 'bell-ringer' activities, 'exit tickets' and to pose open-ended questions to students. Teachers can customize each Padlet's appearance and privacy settings and even moderate student posts. It can be used to share student drawings and mental models" (Chandler, 2015).

Google Forms

With Google Forms teachers can create online surveys, quizzes, questionnaires, and much more. Teachers can create a form using a number of different types of questions, and share the form with students and parents. Use the form to collect data and then analyze the results. Schools have used Google Forms in countless of ways. For example, teachers can use Google Forms to create online quizzes, tests, exit tickets, student/parent surveys, and so forth. Teachers can also collect data from the quizzes, tests, and exit tickets and then use those data to drive instruction.

TED Ed Video Library

The library which is housed on YouTube features a wide variety of educational videos curated specifically for educators. These TED Ed videos are explanatory tutorials and animations that cover a number of topics. Many of these videos are created by teachers in partnership with professional animators ensuring both content accuracy and a pleasant viewing experience (Ed Tech Team, 2014).

Twiducate

Twiducate is a potential social media "solution for elementary and secondary students. Rather than having your students sign up and enter an email address, teachers can sign up and create a class code. Using this code, your students log in to your class network. Here, they can answer questions, collaborate on problems, and even embed pictures and videos. As a teacher you have full control over the network" (Twiducate, 2012).

Three Ring

This is a digital tool that allows students to create online portfolios. Three Ring "allows teachers and students to document anything, organize it in seconds, and have it seamlessly available at school and at home." Features of this tool are: "Capture photos, videos, audio, and notes from class, enjoy unlimited storage, align your artifacts by student, subject, and tag/standard, secure permissions based sharing to all the right stakeholders and only the right stakeholders, and access your artifacts in the app and on the web" (Three Ring, 2015).

Permission Click

Teachers have the ability to create digital permission slips for parents to sign digitally. Users can submit permission slips to administration for approval; events can be accepted or rejected with comments. Parents can digitally approved the event using any device. Teachers can receive instant notification of new approvals and events are securely archived and searchable (Permission Click, 2015).

Easy Voice Recorder

"Easy Voice Recorder is a fun, simple and easy to use audio & voice recorder. Use it to reliably record your meetings, personal notes, classes, and more, with no time limits! Some of its features include: Share and manage your recordings easily, and back them up to your PC; Record in the background and control the recorder with a home screen widget" (Easy Voice recorder, 2015).

Tape-a-Talk

Tape-a-Talk is a high-quality voice recorder designed for simplicity and is able to record voice notes/voice memos/audio even when the display is off. Some of its features include: "Record in high or low quality, in background and with pause function; backwards/fast-forward during a recording as on your dictation machine; Record by Widget; Send, rename and delete recordings; 'Fast' Send, now with custom mail recipients; upload to Dropbox, FTP, etc." (Tape-a-Talk, 2014).

Prezi ($$)

"Prezi is a powerful web tool that allows you to create visually appealing presentations. Teachers can start with a professionally designed template from Prezi's library then use images, text, videos and zooming features to enhance your presentation. Teachers can also collaborate with colleagues to build presentations. Prezi is available on iOS and Android so it can be used to create or edit presentations on the go, then auto-sync across all your devices with ease" (Ed Tech Team, 2015).

Haiku Deck

Haiku Deck is a "presentation tool for teachers and students. Teachers can use it to visually narrate stories. The site offers a variety of pre-made themes and templates to choose from. Teachers can search Haiku's image library for images which can be included in presentations. Users can also upload their own personal images. Stories that teachers have created on Haiku Deck can also be shared on social networking websites such as Facebook and Twitter. Lastly, stories created on Haiku Deck can be exported as PPT files or embedded in blog posts" (Ed Tech Team, 2015).

Glogster ($$)

"Digital storytelling is a powerful way to share and engage with information. Students and teachers can save time and effort by bringing stories to life on a single page. Combine text, images, videos and audio with the drag and drop Glogster tool, then instantly share the output with others" (Glogster Edu, 2015).

HSTRY

HSTRY is a web tool that allows teachers and students to create multimedia timelines in class. Users simply need to sign up either as a teacher or a student and choose the timeline the individual would like to work on. Users can add images, videos, and audio to their timeline. An additional benefit of HSTRY is it will allow teachers to create a classroom and then invite students to join it. Once a classroom is created, teachers can then share timelines with their students and view timelines that are created by students. Lastly, teachers can add additional interactivity by inserting questions for students to answer (HSTRY, 2015).

The Getty

"The Getty makes available, without charge, all available digital images to which the Getty holds the rights or that are in the public domain to be used for any purpose. No permission is required. Currently, there are more than 99,000 images from the J. Paul Getty Museum and the Getty Research Institute available through the Open Content Program" (The Getty, 2015).

Flashcard Hero (free version)

"Make your own flash cards and take the pressure out of test preparation. Flashcard Hero keeps track of what facts students already know so teachers can focus on what students don't know and save a lot of time. Beyond the average-vocab-app: Flashcard Hero was made for those teachers who want to fit more than a few words on each card. You can add lists and use text formatting to structure your content. Cards even expand as you add more text so students can take notes during class and turn them into study cards later. All decks can easily be shared with others via the web" (Flashcard Hero, 2016).

Google Goggles

"Search by taking a picture: point a mobile phone camera at a painting, a famous landmark, a barcode or QR code, a product, or a popular image. If Goggles finds it in its database, it will provide the user with useful information. Goggles can read text in English, French, Italian, German, Spanish, Portuguese, Russian, and Turkish, and translate it into other languages. Goggles also works as a barcode/QR code scanner" (Google Goggles, 2014).

Features include: "Scan barcodes, scan QR codes, Recognize famous landmarks, translate by taking a picture of foreign text, recognize paintings, books, DVD's, CD's, and almost any 2D image" (Google Goggles, 2014).

Edusight Notes

Edusight Notes is based on the premise that assessment is more than just a grade. Their goal is to capture learning when it happens. This app lets teachers quickly "capture anecdotal evidence. Make note of important behavior or character development for all your students. Store exemplars of student work to guide your assessment practice. All your notes and observations are organized by student in a handy timeline view. Reflect on students' progress by reviewing evidence of their learning" (Edusight Notes, 2015).

CarQuiz Math Game (Apple)

"CarQuiz is a math game for kids, where the player races around a track answering math equations. CarQuiz builds skills in addition, subtraction, multiplication and division. The objective of the game is to get as many correct answers as possible. CarQuiz combines elements of a racing game with learning math. It is designed to be challenging as the player progresses. CarQuiz supports sharing by offering five different profiles to track player progress" (CarQuiz Math Game, 2015).

Tellagami ($$)

"Tellagami is a mobile app that lets you create and share an animated Gami video. A Gami can be an exciting tweet or status update. It can be a fun way to tell a story. It can be a homework assignment notification. It could serve as a guide on a digital field trip. It could be the tool teachers use to open their class or provide students with a Do Now as they enter the classroom" (Telllagami Edu, 2015).

Google Docs

"Google Docs is an online word processor that lets you create and format text documents and collaborate with other people in real time." Here's what you can do with Google Docs: "upload a Word document and convert it to a Google document, add flair and formatting to your documents by adjusting margins, spacing, fonts, and colors, invite other people to collaborate on a document with you, giving them editing rights, comment or view access, collaborate online in real time and chat with other collaborators" (Overview of Google Docs, Sheets, and Slides, 2015).

Purpose Games

A website devoted to helping students learn. Teachers can create a quiz or study guide using gamification. The site offers different types of quizzes/study guides: Image Quiz, Multiple Choice Quiz or a Shape quiz. Teachers can also create groups for each of the games as well as a Play List (Purpose Games, 2015).

CrashCourse

A YouTube channel "tons of awesome courses in one awesome channel: Hank Green teaches you Anatomy & Physiology; Phil Plait teaches you Astronomy; Craig Benzine teaches you U.S. Government and Politics. . . .
"Check out the playlists for past courses in World History, Biology, Literature, Ecology, Chemistry, Psychology, and US History" (CrashCourse, 2015). An entertaining look at multiple lessons and subjects.

Summary

In the lesson plan provided in table 8.1, students are using the digital tool Glogster. Glogster will allow students to make an online/digital poster. This lesson also has students working in groups and collaborating. The groups of students will also need to critically think and assess the information they would like to display on the Glogster poster. Once they do this they then need to create the online poster. As you can see students are asked to use twenty-first-century skills: collaboration, team work, and critical thinking. They are also asked to complete work that has varying levels of cognitive consumption (Webb's DOK): recall the facts from earlier lessons; apply the skills of spacing, margins, colors, and layout to maximize the digital poster board; and think strategically about what content to use and how to lay the content out on the Glogster poster.

REDESIGN

The Redesign stage asks the teacher to step beyond the Assimilation stage of technology integration. Here the assignment is simply using technology

Table 8.1. Assimilate Lesson Plan

Title of Lesson: Desperately Needed . . . Inventors!!		
Date: 12/15/15	Course: 4th Grade LA	Time Allotment: 2 class periods
Targets for the Lesson		
Common Core Standard(s)/State Standard(s): CCSS.ELA-Literacy SL 4.5 Add audio recordings and visual displays to presentations when appropriate to enhance the development of main ideas or themes.		**21st Century Skills:** ☐ Information/Media Skills X Critical/Creative Thinking Skills

Learning Target(s):
  1) I can plan and organize a layout for a digital poster board.
  2) I can apply spacing, margins, colors and layout to maximize the digital poster board.
  3) I can list critical information pertaining to inventions.
		X Collaboration/ Communication Skills
		
		X Creating/Innovating

Evidence of Mastery: Digital Poster		**Cognitive Consumption** X Recall & Reproduction X Skills & Concepts
Resources: Notes regarding inventions Internet sources Glogster		X Strategic Thinking ☐ Extended Thinking

Lesson Sequence / Activity: After completing the unit on Inventions, the students will show mastery of both the Inventions content as well as CCSS EL 4.5 (visual displays to presentation to enhance the development of main ideas or themes). Students will:

1) Review their invention material,

2) Become acquainted with their group members and roles,

3) As a group collaborate to determine what information and items need to be listed on the digital poster board,

4) Work collaboratively using Glogster to create a digital poster board representing their inventions,

5) Work as a team, using the provided rubric, to determine the overall quality of the digital poster board, and

6) Present their invention information to the class using Glogster.

to assimilate a current pen-and-pencil task to the Redesign stage and asks the teacher to use the technology for the purpose of allowing students to engage in, and access the content in a new way that would not be possible with a paper and pencil.

For example, the Assimilation stage would have a teacher use Google Doc's to replace the spelling workbook in a second-grade classroom. The teacher could view each student's work and grade the work on the Google Doc. The Redesign stage would then ask for greater task complexity. At this stage the teacher could ask that three students in second grade form a group. They would each log on to Google, view the words (as they would in the Assimilation stage), and then they would collaborate online. Each student could work on the same sentence for the same work at the same time. They would have the ability to instant message one another and make comments on completed sentences. This could all happen in real time without the students sitting by each other.

Below is a list of digital tools that teachers can use at the Redesign stage of the ART model.

Redesign Digital Tools

Global iBook

"The Global iBook is an ongoing project set up by Meg Wilson, a special education teacher and Apple Distinguished Educator. This project brings classrooms around the world together to create an ebook in the app Book Creator for iPad. The aim is to give students and educators from across the world the opportunity to collaborate and create something unique and creative using only the iPad" (A Global iBook, 2013).

Comic Strip It (lite)

"With Comic Strip It users can make compelling comic strips and story boards instantly. Use images from your gallery or take new photos directly into a comic strip, then position, resize, and rotate each frame. Add captions, titles, speech bubbles and more. Apply image effects to each frame to create a comic-book feel, then share via any social platforms" (Comic Strip It! [lite], 2014).

Curriculet

"Embed a layer of questions, quizzes, and rich media annotations into any reading assignment. Track mastery of literacy skills and Common Core standards in real-time" (Curriculet, 2015).

YummyMath

"The site mixes videos, images, and real-world challenges that get students thinking about where math fits into their day-to-day lives. The site divides posts by age group, genre, and the type of math on display. The website often posts activities that relate to current holidays or something going on in pop culture, making it easy to tie in the activities with something your students are interested in" (Hicks, 2015).

MathsFrame

MathsFrame is a UK website with nearly two hundred interactive math games for students to play. The games focus on a variety of math types and levels. Games like Maths Invaders and Mine Mayhem use a Star Wars-esque set up to get students invested in getting arithmetic problems right. Other games more directly tackle real-world situations like the ones on Reading Scales and Adding Time. There is also a section that organizes the games by Common Core standards (MathsFrame, 2012).

Get the Math

"*Get the Math* is about algebra in the real world. See how professionals use math in music, fashion, videogames, restaurants, basketball, and special effects. Then take on interactive challenges related to those careers" (Get the Math, 2015).

Duolingo.com

Foreign language goes gamification. Learn any language, anytime via videos and games (Duolingo, 2015).

Khan Academy

Khan Academy is a nonprofit educational organization created in 2006 by educator Salman Khan to provide "a free, world-class education for anyone, anywhere." Khan Academy produces micro lectures in the form of YouTube videos. In addition to micro lectures, the website features practice exercises and tools for educators. All resources are available for free to anyone around the world (Khan Academy, 2016).

Kahoot!

Kahoot! is a game-based educational platform that leaves students begging for more. "With a refreshingly new take on introducing a subject and formative assessment through quizzing, collaboration and presentation of content. Kahoot! initiates peer-led discussions, with students left on the edge of their seats" (Kahoot!, 2014).

The Answer Pad (TAP)

TAP has "two cool tools with one easy to use platform. A Student response system together with a grading solution for your quizzes! It's all about student engagement & timely feedback" (The Answer Pad, 2015).

Nearpod

Teachers create or download an interactive multimedia presentation. The presentations are then shared with students via an interactive lesson. The teacher has the ability to control the lesson or activity in real time. Students interact with the lesson and submit responses. Nearpod then will monitor and measure student's results and can aggregate or disaggregate student data (Nearpod, 2015).

Google Forms + Flubaroo

Teachers use Google Forms to create a quiz or a test. Google Forms offers multiple types of questions such as matching, T/F, short answer, etc. Teachers can use a Google Add On, called Flubaroo, to grade the quiz or test. Flubaroo will create a spread sheet of data which will include each student's response to each question plus much more. Flubaroo also has the ability to e-mail each student his or her individual score as soon as Flubaroo grades the assessments.

Easy Portfolio ($$)

This app allows teachers "to create various classes and portfolios, while maintaining its easily navigated layout. This app allows for audio recordings, video, text, and pictures to be captured directly into the portfolio. Documents can also be imported from Dropbox" (Nichols, 2013).

OpenSchool ePortfolio

This is a digital tool that allows students to create online portfolios. "Use OpenSchool ePortfolio to create and manage digital portfolios for your entire class! Create and assign student projects, take pictures, video and audio recordings of student work and upload them right to a student's ePortfolio, use the built-in rubric maker to view Common Core State Standards, as well as other standards, that are pre-leveled, to facilitate authentic assessment" (OpenSchool ePortfolio, 2014).

Presentious

"Presentious turns your live presentations into recordings that pair your audio with each slide. It's a powerful format that combines the narrative structure of slides with the context of commentary" (Presentious, 2015).

Noteflight

Noteflight is an online music writing application that lets you create, view, print, and hear professional quality music notation right in your web browser. Write music on your computer, tablet or smartphone, share with other users, or embed in your own pages. Students can use it to learn about the basics of music composition and write sheet music (A Must Have Chrome App for Music, 2015).

"Note flight has several features that enable students to work on music scoring and composition across different devices. Students collaborate with each other to work on small projects or to share scores. Lastly, students can also use it to import and export music XML files or use it to embed music in a classroom blog or website" (A Must Have Chrome App for Music, 2015).

HaikuJam

"Create poetry and photo stories with others from around the world! As seen in Forbes, The Times of India, Zee News and IBN Live." With Haiku-Jam students can: "co-create poetry and photo stories, JAM with friends in circles, JAM with strangers around the world, explore content according to different tags, view a live feed of all concluded collaborations, view a featured feed of entries handpicked by the HaikuJam team, share collaborations through Facebook, Twitter and email" (Haiku Jam, 2015).

Educanon

Digital tool that allows teachers to insert questions into videos. The tool allows teachers to insert multiple choice, fill in the blank, check all that apply, and extended response questions. The tool allows teachers to use video to differentiate content to engage students, promote self-paced learning (via pause and rewind), and insert formative assessment as well as allowing for student explanations and teacher remediation (Educanon, 2015).

Google Slides

Google Slides is an online presentation software that allows the user to develop presentations, much like PowerPoint, online, save them online or download them. Also, Google Slides allows the user to collaborate with other users in real time while creating the presentation (Google Slides, 2015).

ZeeMaps

ZeeMaps allows users to create interactive maps for any region around the world. Users can place a "marker" anywhere in the world as many times as they like. Users can add images and videos to any marker. ZeeMaps also allows for three different levels of access: viewer, member, and administrator (ZeeMaps, 2015).

ScribbleMaps

A digital tool that allows users to create interactive maps. With the map users can place "markers" anywhere in the world. Users can overlay images, place text, draw shapes, use distance and area calculators, and embed images and PDFs (Scribblemaps, 2015).

Google Docs + Read&Write

"Read&Write for Google™ offers a range of powerful support tools to help students gain confidence with reading and writing, including: Hear words, passages, or whole documents read aloud with easy-to-follow dual color highlighting, see the meaning of words explained with text and picture dictionaries, hear text translated into other languages, turn words into text as you speak, and simplify and summarize text on web pages" (Read&Write for Google, 2015).

Halftone2 (Apple app)

Halftone2 makes it easy to create comic and scrap books with your images. Choose a page layout, apply photo filters, position captions, add speech and thought balloons, place some WHAMs, BAMs, and POWs, mix in a few sound effects, and share your creation as an image, multi-page document, or high-definition video. There's no faster or more fun way to share your stories. With Halftone2 students and teachers can use: captions and balloons, stamps, photo panels, page options, video, editing, and output/sharing (Halftone2, 2015).

Anatomy 4D (Apple)

"Through this free app and a simple printed image, Anatomy 4D transports students and teachers into an interactive 4D experience of human anatomy. Visually stunning and completely interactive, Anatomy 4D uses augmented reality and other cutting edge technologies to create the perfect vehicle for 21st century education.

"With this digital tool students can: learn about and explore the human body and heart in intricate detail, highlight various organ systems individually, change the view back and forth between a male and female body, zoom in to experience each organ or body part in-depth, and use new image targets including the new heart target" (Anatomy 4D, 2015).

Clarisketch

"Clarisketch is an interesting app that enables you to create animated sketches by combining speech, drawing and photos. As a teacher, you can use Clarisketch to create flipped classroom videos, explain a complex process or illustrate a given topic using both annotated commentary and recorded audio. You will be able to walk the students through your explanations using features such as highlights, drawings and audio prompts" (Clarisketch, 2015).

Riddle

"Riddle is a web tool for teachers that allow them to create their own interactive quizzes, lists, polls, and much more. Riddle's goal is to provide best-in-class tools that make creating interactive content simple, so teachers can concentrate on the content instead of worrying about the tools" (7 New Educational Web Tools for Teachers, 2015). The platform is device agnostic, thus it can be used on any digital device with a web browser. The teacher can provide the riddle to users via embedding a link to the class website and posting it on Facebook or Twitter. Riddle will also provide the teacher with vital stats regarding student and whole class achievement.

PowToon ($$)

Create engaging presentation or story boards using this digital tool. "PowToon features an easy 'Drag and Drop' user interface, pre-designed templates, and a variety of style libraries. Each 'slide' is treated as a scene in the storyline of your presentation or video. Drag and drop characters and props onto your slide then assign it an animation" (Four Useful Chromebook Apps for Digital Storytelling, 2015).

Socrative

"Socrative, a digital tool, that lets teachers engage and assess their students with educational activities on tablets, laptops and smartphones. Through the use of real time questioning, instant result aggregation and visualization, teachers can gauge the whole class' current level of understanding" (Socrative, 2015).

Canva

"Canva provides teachers and students with a simple new way to design. Its drag and drop functionality enables them to create presentations, posters, one-page documents, and social media posts. With more than 1 million photos, icons, and layouts, students are empowered with a design tool that allows them to explore, engage, and innovate in new ways" (Canva for Education, 2015).

Biteslide (free—$$)

Biteslide is a tool that "teachers and students can use to present and create slidebooks. A Slidebook is a presentation that embeds a blend of different multimedia materials that include images, videos, and text. Biteslide is web-based and does not require any software installation. Students can upload images and annotate them with text, add borders and stickers. They can also add clips and videos from YouTube. When students are done they can download and print their finalized work" (Biteslide, 2015).

Edulastic (free—$$)

Edulastic is an "assessment solution that enables teachers to gauge students' progress in meeting Common Core-aligned standards on any device. They can create a free account and utilize real-time insights into student performance, day by day, to provide immediate feedback and intervention. Teachers can create formative assessments tailored to their students' learning needs with interactive, technology-enhanced items and thousands of high-quality questions in the style of the PARCC and Smarter Balanced assessments. The cloud-based platform provides real-time, reliable Common Core proficiency reports by student, class, school, and district throughout the year" (Edulastic, 2015).

Newsela (free—$$)

"Newsela publishes daily news articles at 5 reading levels from grades 3–12 to drive gains in literacy. Explore a library of high-quality, engaging nonfiction that you need to meet the new, rigorous demands of the Common Core. Newsela adapts to the reading level of your students while empowering them to adjust the complexity of the text. Students are empowered to build background knowledge through multiple re-readings and learn to apply strategies like highlighting and annotation to digital text" (Newsela, 2014).

VideoNotes

VideoNotes "enables you to: Watch videos and take notes at the same time, on the same screen, keep the same shortcuts to play/pause your video while writing notes, automatically synchronize your notes and video. Just click on a line of your notes to jump to the related part of the video. Everything is automatically stored in your Google Drive, to access them everywhere" (VideoNot.es, 2013).

Google Doc + Kaizena

Kaizena is an add-on that allows users to add audio/voice comments to student work on a Google Doc. Teachers also have the ability to link resources to highlighted text as well as write a text comment to the student or class (Kaizena About, 2015).

Quiver

"The Quiver App combines physical coloring from 'back in the day' with state of the art augmented reality technology to bring you and your children an extraordinarily magical experience. Every colored page comes to life in its uniquely colored way, giving the artist an immediate and special sense of ownership and pride! Not only is the app incredibly fun, but it is also a great tool for developing skills and knowledge on various topics" (Quiver, 2015).

Summary

In the lesson presented in table 8.2, students are asked to use Educanon to show mastery of a movie they are watching. The students are watching the movie after they have read the book. Students will also use the digital tool Prezi to complete a group presentation on the book/movie. Students are asked to complete a number of twenty-first-century skills: students will use information and media skills to complete the Educanon assessment throughout the movie; students will critically think to answer the questions via Educanon as well as determine content to be included on the Prezi; students will also collaborate and work in teams to complete the Prezi.

Table 8.2. Redesign Lesson Plan

Title of Lesson: The Outsiders Movie (EduCannon)		
Date: December 1, 2015	Course: 8th Grade English/Lit	Time Allotment: 3 days

Targets for the Lesson	
Common Core Standard(s) / State Standard(s): CCSS.ELA-Literacy.RL.8.1 • Cite the textual evidence that most strongly supports an analysis of what the text says explicitly as well as inferences drawn from the text. • Write arguments to support claims with clear reasons and relevant evidence	*21st Century Skills:* **X** Information/Media Skills **X** Critical/Creative Thinking Skills
Learning Target(s): 1) I can analyze multi-media data and cite evidence to support personal opinions and inferences. 2) I can clearly write and state an argument citing the appropriate evidence.	**X** Collaboration/ Communication Skills ☐ Creating/Innovating
Evidence of Mastery: 1) Completion of the Educanon assessment for the video of the "Outsiders." 2) Successfully completed group presentation, using Prezi, outlining the essential themes of the movie/book.	*Cognitive Consumption* **X** Recall & Reproduction **X** Skills & Concepts
Resources: 1) Individual digital devices 2) "Nothing Gold Can Stay" by Robert Frost 3) *Outsiders* Movie 4) Educanon 5) Google Slides	**X** Strategic Thinking **X** Extended Thinking

Lesson Sequence / Activity:
1) After reading the book and completing the previous lessons students will:
2) watch the movie, *Outsiders*, on their individual device,
3) students will answer questions via Educanon throughout the movie,
4) work in groups to complete a presentation (Google Slides) outlining the themes of the movie/book while citing evidence to support those themes.
5) Educanon Questions:
6) Can you recall what happened to Pony on his way home from the movies? (DOK 1)
7) Distinguish between Dally's approach to Cherry and Marcia's with Ponyboy. (DOK 2)
8) Connect what happened to Johnny prior to the time of this story and hypothesize how this may have influenced him.
9) List the reasons Ponyboy applies to the separation of the Greaser's and the Soc's. (DOK1)
10) List and critique Johnny and Ponyboy's reasons for going to Jay's Mountain. (DOK 3)
11) Based on the readings and movie, make observations (citing evidence) that would describe Johnny's relationship with his parents. (DOK 2)
12) State the reasons for Johnny's anger regarding his haircut. (DOK 1)
13) Describe Johnny's reaction when his mother visited him in the hospital. (DOK 1)
14) Using context clues, infer potential reasons that Dally felt responsible for Johnny's fate (DOK 2).
15) Assess, citing evidence, Ponyboy's evolving opinion of the Soc's from the beginning of the movie to the end. (DOK 3)
16) Apply the concept of Police Assisted Suicide (using credible web sources) to Dally's robbery of the grocery store.
17) Analyze the Poem, "Nothing Gold Can Stay" and connect three concepts from the poem to the movie/book. (DOK 4)

Also, students are asked to complete a number of tasks that vary in cognitive consumption: students are asked to recall facts from the book and the movie; students are asked to apply their skills to the Prezi and concepts (liturgical) in the Prezi; students are asked to think strategically in completing the Prezi and answering some of the Educanon questions; students are asked to complete extended thinking tasks in the Educanon assessment.

TRANSFIGURE

In the Transfigure stage teachers provide learning opportunities that schools could not imagine let alone accomplish a decade ago due to the power of the now available digital devices and tools. At this stage teachers take a learning opportunity or task and make it something much more engaging, exciting, and beautiful than it was before the current technology became available.

Quite often the conversation regarding technology in schools is trapped in the wrong subject. The talk is about "does the technology work" as a fix for the old method (Assimilation). It ought to be about developing and choosing between visions of how this immensely powerful technology can support the invention of powerful new forms of learning to serve levels of expectation higher than anything imagined in the past (Papert & Caperton, 1999).

Returning to the second-grade spelling example, at this stage, the teacher would allow students to work and collaborate with one another using Google Docs to cover the assigned spelling words. However, the teacher would take an extra step to provide a learning experience that would not be possible without the latest technology to topple the school walls and technect students to learning real-world learning opportunities.

For example, Teacher X would assign the words using Google Docs. Students would collaborate on the words and write sentences using Google Docs. However, the teacher would also arrange, in advance, a digital pen pal with a second-grade class in Mexico. The students would use Google Translate to write their words in Spanish. They would now be able to see, spell, and pronounce the word in Spanish (second grade is a great time to teach foreign languages).

The students would then collaborate with students from Mexico. They would be able to communicate and work together to write sentences for each word in a foreign language with a student from another country without ever leaving their seat.

The Transfigure stage makes this a reality. Below is a list of digital tools that serve the Transfigure stage of the ART model.

Transfigure Digital Tools

Educurious (free—$$)

"Educurious delivers next-generation learning experiences that: increase students' self-confidence as they solve real problems and see the results, expand students' career possibilities by connecting them to renowned experts, equip students with the communication and technology skills they need for college and careers, shift the role of students from passive learners to active collaborators, problem solvers, and contributors, incorporate the technologies students use every day through our blended learning model" (Educurious, 2015).

WeLearnedIt

WeLearnedIt is an easy-to-use project-based learning platform that allows teachers to create and share dynamic assignments, leave meaningful feedback on student work, and allows learners to capture and track their academic growth and achievement over time in digital learning portfolios. WeLearnedIt "embraces project based learning for teachers who want their students to 'think outside the bubble.' Some of the features are: Rubric and Assignment Library, incredibly easy to set up classes, progress reporting, and annotation feature on created content and digital learning portfolios" (We Learned It, 2015).

Google Hangouts

"Google Hangouts is Google's free video-conferencing tool that is available for teachers to use as part of Google Apps for Education. Up to 10 participants can join a Google Hangout at a time. It's a great way to connect your classroom with other classrooms anywhere in the world" (Google Hangouts Guide for Teachers, 2015).

Skype for Education

"Skype for education is dedicated to improving classroom instruction and bringing the world to your classroom. With Skype for Education teachers can collaborate with other classes no matter where they are. Find guest speakers and invite them to your classroom as well as take a virtual field trip anywhere in the world" (Skype for Education, 2015).

ProjectEd

ProjectEd is "crowdsourcing the world's best educational videos. Project Ed helps teachers by providing vocabulary videos that can be used for critical discussions regarding language and meaning, and to teach writing skills like dialoguing, story arts and story boards. Also Project Ed can be used as Project Based Learning where students create Project Ed videos in the classroom and enter the monthly contest" (Educators, 2013).

Blendspace

Blendspace is a "tool for designing learning activities, assessing student knowledge, and tracking student progress. Teachers can 'blend' videos, images, websites, and quizzes into lessons for students. Blendspace also offers a gallery of existing lessons created by teachers for teachers. Blendspace has built-in features that will allow students to add comments regarding the lesson plan and the appropriate learning activity as well as the ability to indicate individual level of understanding. Lastly, Blendspace also offers a lesson-tracking feature that allows teacher to monitor student progress, engagement, and assessment results" (Chandler, 2015).

Book Creator (Windows, Android, or Apple)

Book Creator is the simple way to make your own beautiful e-books, right on your PC or tablet. With over 15 million e-books created so far, Book Creator is ideal for making all kinds of books, including children's picture books, photo books, comic books, journals, textbooks and more. And when you're done, share your book with ease, or even publish it to online book stores! With Book Creator students and teachers can share their book via: e-mail, OneDrive, Google Drive, Dropbox (and more). Provide your students with a voice (Book Creator, 2016).

iBooks Author (Apple)

Students can make their own books. "Start with one of the Apple-designed templates that feature a wide variety of page layouts. Add your own text and images with drag-and-drop ease. Use Multi-Touch widgets to include interactive photo galleries, movies, Keynote presentations, 3D objects, and more. Preview your book on your iPad or Mac at any time. Then submit your finished work to the iBooks Store in a few simple steps" (iBooks Author, 2015).

NowComment

"NowComment makes it easy to have rich, engaging discussions of online documents no matter how large (or small) your class or collaboration group. NowComment . . . lets you quickly see what passages people are commenting on, easily find all the comments on the passages *you're* most interested in, and have unlimited distinct conversations on any sentence and paragraph" (NowComment, 2015). Some important features are: commenting, comment sorting, private reply, teachers can create groups, embed a NowComment document in your class webpage, create blogs from NowComment, highlight text, and so forth. (NowComment, 2015).

Explain Everything ($$)

"Explain Everything is an easy-to-use design, screencasting, and interactive whiteboard tool that lets you annotate, animate, narrate, import, and export almost anything to and from almost anywhere. Create slides, draw in any color, add shapes, add text, and use a laser pointer" (Explain Everything, 2016).

Seesaw (free—$$) (Apple product)

Seesaw is a digital portfolio with powerful tools. Students have the ability to easily collect their own work, organize it within their Seesaw account, make comments on the digital copy of their work, as well as collaborate with their classmates. Teachers have the ability to organize whole class work and individual student work. Students and teachers have the ability to connect each student's digital portfolio with the student's custodial parents. Whenever content is added to an individual student's portfolio a message and link is sent to the parents (Seesaw, n.d.).

EDpuzzle

EDpuzzle allows "teachers to make any video your lesson. Crop a video, explain it with your own voice and embed quizzes at any time. Take any video from YouTube, Khan Academy, Learn Zillion, and the like. Make it perfect for your classroom and more engaging for your students. Make any video a true lesson by making it to the point, personal and effective, plus get all the data about your students so you know if they truly understand the lesson" (EDpuzzle, 2014).

Virtual Debate

The Virtual Debate project infuses technology into an authentic argumentative writing experience by giving students an audience. To do this teachers work with another school and hold a debate. Teachers who wish to participate in the virtual debate will find mini-lessons, anchor charts, and other resources on the project's website. The final debate is judged by experts from around the country and is recorded using Google Hangouts On Air so parents can tune in and see their child's hard work (Figurelli and Franzi, 2015).

Table 8.3. Transfigure Lesson Plan

Title of Lesson: Illegal Immigration Experience		
Date: December 15, 2015	Course: Spanish	Time Allotment: 4 Days
Targets for the Lesson		
Common Core Standard(s) / State Standard(s): N/A		***21st Century Skills:***
Learning Target(s): 1) I can read and interpret news stories in Spanish. 2) I can research, plan, and organize a debate on illegal immigration. 3) I can create, using Canva, a persuasive brochure defending my position on illegal immigration. 4) I can utilize 21st century tools to communicate and collaborate with students in Mexico.		X Information/MediaSkills ❏ Critical/Creative Thinking Skills X Collaboration/ Communication Skills ❏ Creating/Innovating
Evidence of Mastery: 1) Brochure 2) Debate 3) Conversation, in Spanish, with Mexican students using Google Hangouts		***Cognitive Consumption*** ❏ Recall & Reproduction X Skills & Concepts
Resources: 1) Canva 2) Google Translate 3) Google Hangouts 4) Google Docs		X Strategic Thinking X Extended Thinking
Lesson Sequence / Activity: Day 1 & 2: Students will read articles that are written in Spanish on Google Docs (provided by teacher). Students will access Internet sites (provided by teacher) that are translated in Spanish. Students will use facts from their research to create a persuasive digital brochure using Canva. Day 3: Students will participate in a debate, moderated by the teacher, covering illegal immigration. When the debate is completed the class, using a Google Doc, will collaborate to generate a series of questions to ask students from Mexico regarding the topic of immigration covering their perceptions of immigration and America. Day 4: Using Google Hangouts students will communicate with a classroom from Mexico in Spanish on the topic of immigration. Students will use the questions created the day before on the Google Doc as a starter for the conversation.		

Summary

In the lesson plan provided in table 8.3, students are asked to complete a Spanish assignment using Google Docs, Canva, and Google Hangouts. To complete the assignment students are asked to use a number of twenty-first-century skills: students will use information and media skills via Google Docs, online research, use Canva for creating a brochure, as well as using Google Hangouts. Students are also asked to complete a number of tasks with varying levels of cognitive consumption: they collaborate using Google Doc's; apply skills and concepts using Canva; utilize strategic thinking in planning and participating in the debate; and extend their thinking during the debate as well as participate in a Google Hangout.

There are a number of digital tools that can be used to provide students with the twenty-first-century skills they will need. The tools found in this chapter are just the tip of the iceberg. Many more can be found and many more will be created. The key is to stay updated to the technologies that are being used by both businesses and students. The goal is to prepare students to be successful in their world, not ours. Therefore, it is imperative that teachers use tools that are germane to students and business.

9

✛

Planning Tips

The past two chapters have explained the Martin ART model, provided tools for each stage, as well as a lesson plan for each stage. Hopefully, you have now begun to identify different lesson plans or curricular units you would like to reform using the ART model to integrate the appropriate technology.

This reform movement is best if it is not done alone and in isolation. This chapter will discuss and provide research-proven best practices for professional development. Then it will outline a step-by-step process for schools to use when planning a school-wide professional development initiative.

THE NEED FOR PROFESSIONAL DEVELOPMENT

Professional development is the oil to a school's engine. It is what makes the school run. Professional development can be defined as "the continuous process of acquiring new knowledge and skills that relate to one's profession, job responsibilities, or work environment" (Human Resources—Professional Development and Evaluation Programs, 2015).

In today's turbulent and constantly evolving education world, professional development is a must for schools if they want to be successful. Federal and state mandates are constantly barraging educators and schools. If a school and a teacher want to successfully change to meet the demands of the new federal and state mandates, the twenty-first-century student, and the twenty-first-century economy, then high-quality professional development is needed.

However, all schools have some form of professional development and many schools are unsuccessful. This is because, while professional development is being used, many schools are using it inappropriately and ineffectively. Due to this, professional development, in many instances, has received negative criticism from the teachers themselves.

PROFESSIONAL DEVELOPMENT GONE WRONG!

In Chicago in 2014, teachers at a professional development session were videotaped. Unfortunately, the video tape revealed a professional development leader talking to a group of professional teachers as if they were kindergartners. The teachers all sat in seats and recited each sentence after the moderator. What is worse, the moderators were consultants who had been flown in from California and the United Kingdom (Strauss, 2014). When the video was released to the public, it, shockingly, received a great deal of attention. Unfortunately, it was mostly negative feedback. But that negativity was sound. As a professional, it was both painful and embarrassing to watch other professionals being taught and treated this way. Sadly, as many reports of professional development have pointed out—on the whole, professional development is handled poorly!

INEFFECTIVE PROFESSIONAL DEVELOPMENT

Due to the turbulent educational world most of us work in today, special emphasis has been placed on professional development. There has been a great deal of research surrounding the concept and implementation. Because of this emphasis, research has provided insight into what poor and ineffective professional development consists of. Researchers have determined three features of ineffective professional development: fragmentation, lack of implementation, and a lack of teacher centeredness (Telese, 2012).

Fragmentation refers to the perception of teachers that professional development is fragmented, it comes and goes on a need-to-know basis determined by the school leadership. It can be characterized as the "one size fits all," the "one shot," or the fix-'em-up experience (Bissonnette and Caprino, 2014). It isn't consistent nor does it address individual teacher's needs.

Lack of implementation can be described as not allowing individual teachers to set goals for their professional development, not allowing for educators, in general, to celebrate their achievements, accomplishments, or efforts (Bissonnette and Caprino, 2014). Quite often schools lack a comprehensive plan for providing professional development that meets both the teacher's and the school's needs via an ongoing process of learning.

Lack of teacher centeredness denotes the idea that teachers are not at the center or have little control of the learning he or she is to provide. Quite often professional development takes the form of a top-down functional silo, which treats teachers as passive participants (Bissonnette and Caprino, 2014). All too often schools turn to consultants as opposed to mining their own gold.

SO, THE FIX IS . . .

Since research has been able to point out what ineffective professional development is, then the fix should be easy. Simply do the opposite of what is ineffective. That is true to a certain degree. Certainly schools would like to avoid the pitfalls that are clearly identified in the research. However, high-quality professional development consists of more than that.

Thomas Guskey, a well-known author of professional development, has published a number of works on the subject. According to Guskey (1995), high-quality professional development is driven from individualized personal reflection, fills a need for the educator, provides choice for staff members, is relevant and job embedded, and takes place in a social and collaborative environment.

In concordance with the findings of Guskey, Learning Forward, a nationally recognized school reform organization, conducted research on the subject of professional development and developed national standards for professional development: learning communities, leadership, resources, data, learning designs, implementation, and outcomes. In short, professional development should be done in collaboration with other educators, have leaders who create support systems, provide the appropriate resources, be based on multiple sets of data, integrate theories of adult learning, provide a sustained learning experience, and align the outcomes with educator performance (Standards for Professional Learning, n/a).

Armed with this knowledge schools should be able to tailor a professional development plan that fits the needs of the collective body and individual educator. To help illustrate this point, below is an example outline of a professional development plan (see figure 9.1):

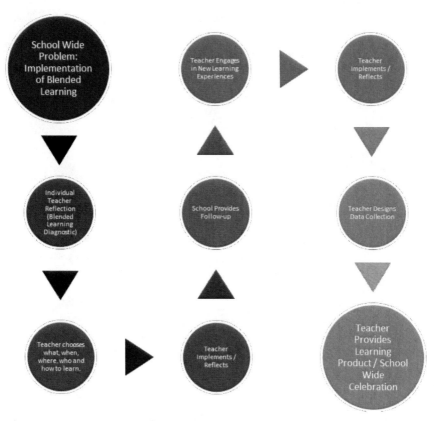

Figure 9.1.   Description: Professional Development Outline

1. The school initiates the move to one-to-one and blended learning. This is done in collaboration with community members, business owners, and the teaching staff.

2. Teacher completes the ART Model Diagnostic Assessment. Teacher reflects on his or her knowledge, skills of the students, and the results of the diagnostic.

3. Based on data from step 2, the teacher chooses what he or she would like to learn (Tools for A, R, or T phase and how to use them, twenty-first-century skills, or cognitive consumption). Here the teacher will also decide if he or she will use learning in groups, when, where, and how the learning will take place.

4. School provides calendar of learning events for the entire year before. For example, teachers who are in the Acclimate stage can meet on the first Tuesday of the month, either before school, after school, or view an online webinar. During that time, teachers are provided with the resources to learn to use the tools that fall under Acclimate.

Teachers are also provided with lesson plan examples to see how the tools have been used. The teacher then is encouraged to go out into the classroom and try what he or she has learned. This can be done alone or with another teacher or a curriculum coach. The teacher reflects on the classroom implementation. On the third Tuesday of the month the school provides an opportunity for the teachers in the Acclimate stage to meet again. Here they discuss what they did, what worked, and what didn't work. Teachers share skill, knowledge, and lesson plans with one another. Teachers are encouraged to once again go out and use the tools in the classroom, now armed with their new knowledge. The second month will see the same group of teachers meet on the first Tuesday, learn some new tools, use them in the classroom, reflect, and meet on the third Tuesday and so on. This cycle will take place throughout the year. Teachers, in discussion with direct administration, are able to move to the next stage in the ART model when ready.

5. Teachers, in conjunction with other teachers and administration begin to develop data collection methods to assess their growth in their chosen area of study. Teachers, in conjunction with other teachers and administration, also develop a product to show off and highlight what they learned throughout the year.

6. School, teachers, and administrators alike present their data findings and product to their chosen learning groups at the end of the year. This should be treated as a celebration. Schools can also elect to provide both continuing education units (CEUs) and college credit for the time and product.

Again, this is just a rough outline of what a professional development plan could look like. It is easy to recognize the key features of effective professional development. This plan is based on individual teacher reflection and data. The plan will fit the needs of each individual teacher. It is both relevant and job embedded. Everything the teacher learns can be used in class the very next day.

Teachers also have the choice in what they learn, as well as how, where, and when they will learn. The school leaders have provided a professional development plan that is purposeful, structured, and continuous. The plan allows for digital and personnel resources. Teachers have an opportunity to reflect on implementation with other teachers and learn from one another.

Professional development, when done in a manner similar to this, has a greater chance of impacting more teachers and indirectly improving student achievement.

10

✛

A Word of Caution

It is appropriate here to take a moment to slow down and provide cautionary advice. It is easy for schools to get caught up in the hype of technology integration, one-to-one initiatives, and blended learning. However, as earlier chapters have pointed out, going fast can slow a school down. This chapter will provide a word of caution to schools as they travel down this path. While the path is worth traveling, fully preparing for the travel before one actually starts traveling is wise.

DO TODAY'S STUDENTS PREFER LOW TECH?

Districts, schools, and individual classroom teachers are rushing to find ways to integrate technology in the classroom. Many times, districts rush to get the latest technology in their schools and classrooms. With this rush comes a major learning curve for professionals who are charged with delivering content to students. Can schools and teachers keep up with this fast-paced change?

What's worse is teachers spend time learning to use the new device, begin to implement it, and then it becomes outdated. It becomes a vicious cycle for educators. But with this, teachers and schools are still willing to do it. Sometimes schools and teachers become obsessed with finding new technologies. It's as if, they believe, without it they are irrelevant. That thought is not quite true.

Due to many educators' lack of technological understanding as well as their own personal use of technology, many schools and educators are solely focused on ensuring they have mastered the latest fad. But is that what students want? Are students as excited about the latest fad as schools and educators?

Shockingly, the answer is no. While technology is a part of their world and they use it every day, it is also a part of their lives. Thus, they don't think of it as "special." Schools and educators, on the other hand, do. Because, for many educators, since technology was not a part of their lives, they think it *is* special. In many schools and educators' minds, technology can be the cure all. In many students' eyes, technology is simply day-to-day life.

Educator and blogger Cheryl Mizerny introduced a new concept to her middle school class. The concept was called Genius Hour. During this time students were given the option to learn a skill, create something new, or find a way to help others. What she found was quite surprising. According to Cheryl, when students were given free time to learn what they wanted, less than 15 percent of her students chose anything that involved technology. Instead, they wanted to knit, cook, sew, and decorate cakes (Mizerny, 2014).

How do these opposing views of technology impact classrooms? First, understand that students are not as excited to use technology as schools and educators think. Students, to a certain degree, don't mind low-tech learning opportunities. Educators are focused on providing high-tech learning opportunities. There is a disconnect (see figure 10.1). Certainly, today's students do not want to power off when they walk into schools, but they also don't want a "technology on steroids" classroom.

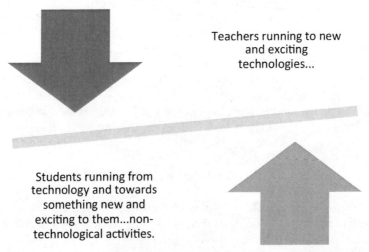

Teachers running to new and exciting technologies...

Students running from technology and towards something new and exciting to them...non-technological activities.

Figure 10.1.   Description: Teacher—Student Technology Disconnect

There needs to be a balance between low-tech learning opportunities and high-tech learning opportunities. Students don't necessarily want schools running to every new digital device that hits the market, but they also don't crave day-to-day math classes using abacus beads and the TI-84 calculator!

As usual, if you ask them, they will tell you. A number of research firms have done just that. The findings are worth reporting. Students report that one-to-one and individualized learning create great learning spaces and opportunities but also require discipline. There is a great deal of freedom and temptation. Temptation turns into distraction, which results in incomplete work and failing grades (Garland, 2014). Ironically, too much freedom can lead to restrictions.

Other students have noted that the online classes, while they are helpful because the video can be watched over and over, are not as rigorous. Students have also commented on the lack of socializing in online classes (Garland, 2014). While students may love socializing on Facebook or Twitter, they miss the personal socialization of school.

Students will also comment on the use of technology in the classroom. Tablets, for example, can be a greater distraction than an educational tool. With the tablet comes distractions such as Minecraft or Netflix (on mute with subtitles). As one young lady stated, "tablets can be used to create a new age of interconnected classrooms of the future—but they are just as likely to turn into procrastination stations" (Shockley, 2015).

What about classroom web pages? Remember, our students grow up viewing websites that are professionally created. Many educator websites are embarrassingly short of student expectations. Social media? Our students use social media for sharing the trivial, not sincere academic conversations (Shockley, 2015). Does social media, such as Twitter, hold great promise? Yes, but students must first be taught how to use it academically.

This is not written to deter any schools or educators from integrating technology into the classroom. Rather, it is a caution to remember that technology is only a tool. And, as such, it should be used correctly and at the appropriate time. Technology is not the solution to education's short comings, rather, it is merely a tool to be used in the solution.

ORWELL AND *1984* VERSUS HUXLEY AND *A BRAVE NEW WORLD*

At 12:01 a.m., January 1, 1984, the world didn't end. The United States somehow managed to be spared from George Orwell's prophetic nightmares. Democracy did indeed reign. In fact, under Ronald Reagan, some would argue, democracy was in full swing.

However, according to Neil Postman (1985), America did not survive another less known prophecy, the Huxleyan prophecy. Aldous Huxley, in his book *A Brave New World,* suggested that America would not fall due to an external oppression, but rather it would be an internal oppression. Huxley, as he saw it, suggested that people would come to love their oppression, to adore the technologies that undo their capacities to think. Huxley's fear wasn't that books would be banned (as Orwell suggested) but rather that no one would want to read one. Huxley feared that our society would have so much information (Orwell suggested the opposite, information would be withheld) available that people would be "reduced to passivity and egoism" (Postman, 1985).

Today's students literally have an infinite amount of information, data, and resources at their fingertips—yet, we fair no better on educational assessments than we did decades ago. Students choose to view multiple formats of media as opposed to reading. This new form of academic media must be mined and used properly in order for it to have a positive impact on student achievement. Students have the ability to create, yet they choose to create the trivial as opposed to the meaningful and purposeful. Too many times we see students create trivial blogs or YouTube videos. Rarely, do we see students harnessing the power of technology to change the lives of students and the world.

This book opened with a teacher and students creating a prosthetic hand for another student. While that is certainly an amazing learning opportunity, it shouldn't be rare. In today's world, with the amount of data, resource, and information we have coupled with the digital tools we possess—it should be the norm!

The word of caution is this: do not forget that technology is merely a tool for educators to provide innovative, engaging, real-world and life-changing learning experiences. However, in order to be real world and life changing, our students need to avoid the malaise as outlined by Huxley and harness the power of today's resources to create and innovate for the greater good.

Students can't be creative, innovative, and great without creative, innovative, and great teachers. Start today!

Appendix A: Lesson Plan Template and Explanation

Title of Lesson:		
Date:	Course:	Time Allotment:

Targets for the Lesson	
Common Core Standard(s) / State Standard(s):	**21st Century Skills:**
Learning Target(s):	❏ Information/Media Skills
Evidence of Mastery:	❏ Critical/Creative Thinking Skills
	❏ Collaboration/ Communication Skills
	❏ Creating/Innovating
Resources:	**Cognitive Consumption**
	❏ Recall & Reproduction
	❏ Skills & Concepts
	❏ Strategic Thinking
	❏ Extended Thinking
Lesson Sequence / Activity:	

Appendix B:
Bloom's Revised Taxonomy

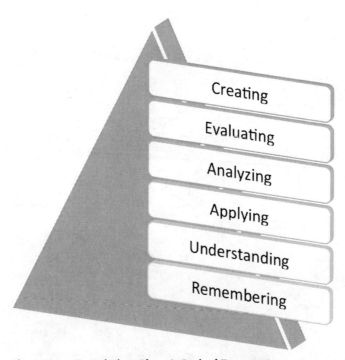

Figure B.1.   Description: Bloom's Revised Taxonomy
Source: http://ww2.odu.edu/educ/roverbau/Bloom/blooms_taxonomy.htm

Appendix C: Webb's Depth of Knowledge (DOK)

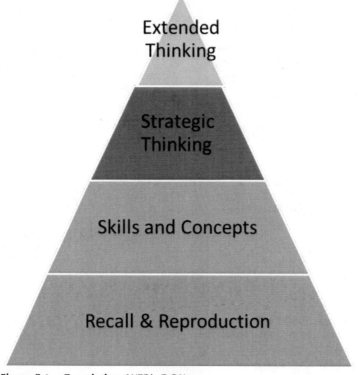

Figure C.1. Description: WEB's DOK

Level 4: Level 4 tasks require the most complex cognitive effort. Students synthesize information from multiple sources, often over an extended period of time, or transfer knowledge from one domain to solve problems in another.

Level 3: At this level of complexity, students must use planning and evidence, and thinking is more abstract.

Level 2: At this level, a student must make some decisions about his or her approach.

Level 1: Tasks at this level require recall of facts or rote application of simple procedures. The task does not require any cognitive effort beyond remembering the right response or formula (Aungst, 2014).

Appendix D: Future Ready Education Environment

Future Ready Schools is a new national effort, supported by hundreds of organizations and federal and state programs, focused on maximizing digital learning opportunities for schools and students. This shift in resource utilization will help districts prepare students for success in college, a career, and citizenship.

A Future Ready school environment is centered on using technology effectively and ensuring that students are future ready. A Future Ready school incorporates five key components into their school environment:

R: Robust and rigorous resources,
E: Engaged students with equitable access,
A: Active parents for deeper engagement,
D: Dedicated educators, and a
Y: "Yes culture" of leadership

To reach this end, the Future Ready movement's efforts is centered on regional summits where participants develop action plans and metrics to measure progress in using digital tools to improve student learning. Summits focus on a comprehensive set of issues that drive student learning, highlight the experiences of districts in each region, and provide school leaders tangible ideas to build capacity in their districts (Future Ready Schools, 2014).

Appendix E:
Twenty-First-Century Skills
and Digital Tools Crosswalk

Chapter 8 of this book is devoted to providing the reader with descriptions of digital tools that fit best in a specific ART category. The reader is left to determine which twenty-first-century skill the tool best fits. This section offers more tools to research and use.

Collaboration	Creativity
1. Edmodo	1. Prezi
2. Google Docs / Sites	2. Appinvetor.org
3. Mapmyself	3. Haiku Deck
4. PB Works	4. Scratch
5. Twiddla	5. Tagxedo
6. Collaborize Classroom	6. VocabGrabber
7. WeKWL	7. Voki
8. Biteslide	8. Museum Box
9. Mural.ly	9. Stencyl
10. Piazza	10. KidsThinkDesign
11. Teen Ink	11. Pixton
Critical Thinking	Communication
1. Edheads	1. Skype
2. Popplet	2. Google Hangouts
3. Scratch	3. Google Docs/Google Dive
4. Webspiration	4. Evernote
5. The Sports Network 2	5. Face Time
6. Think Cerca	6. Wunderlist
7. Read, Write, Think	7. Vyew
8. The Learning Network	8. Co Tweet
9. TweenTribune	9. Backchan.nl
	10. BuddyPress
	11. ClassPager
	12. Diigo

Appendix F:
ART Diagnostic Assessment

For the following scenarios, please read them closely and choose which of the options you would be most comfortable teaching. Beside each scenario is a corresponding letter (P, A, R, and T). Circle the letter that you would feel the most comfortable teaching.

1.

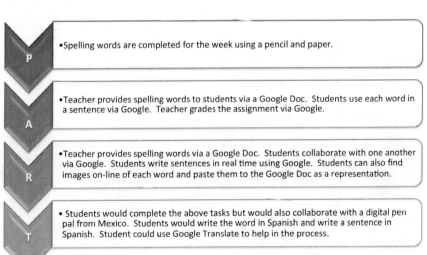

- P
  - •Spelling words are completed for the week using a pencil and paper.

- A
  - •Teacher provides spelling words to students via a Google Doc. Students use each word in a sentence via Google. Teacher grades the assignment via Google.

- R
  - •Teacher provides spelling words via a Google Doc. Students collaborate with one another via Google. Students write sentences in real time using Google. Students can also find images on-line of each word and paste them to the Google Doc as a representation.

- T
  - • Students would complete the above tasks but would also collaborate with a digital pen pal from Mexico. Students would write the word in Spanish and write a sentence in Spanish. Student could use Google Translate to help in the process.

Figure F.1.   Description: ART Model Survey Q1

2.

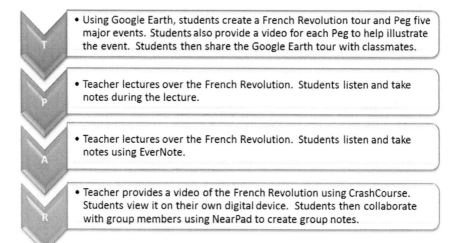

- Using Google Earth, students create a French Revolution tour and Peg five major events. Students also provide a video for each Peg to help illustrate the event. Students then share the Google Earth tour with classmates.

- Teacher lectures over the French Revolution. Students listen and take notes during the lecture.

- Teacher lectures over the French Revolution. Students listen and take notes using EverNote.

- Teacher provides a video of the French Revolution using CrashCourse. Students view it on their own digital device. Students then collaborate with group members using NearPad to create group notes.

Figure F.2.   Description: ART Model Survey Q2

3.

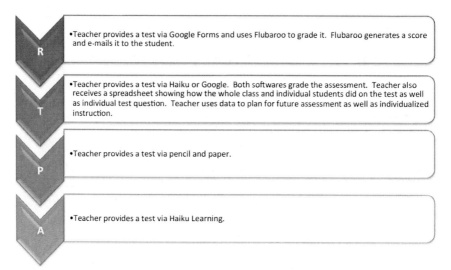

- Teacher provides a test via Google Forms and uses Flubaroo to grade it. Flubaroo generates a score and e-mails it to the student.

- Teacher provides a test via Haiku or Google. Both softwares grade the assessment. Teacher also receives a spreadsheet showing how the whole class and individual students did on the test as well as individual test question. Teacher uses data to plan for future assessment as well as individualized instruction.

- Teacher provides a test via pencil and paper.

- Teacher provides a test via Haiku Learning.

Figure F.3.   Description: ART Model Survey Q3

4.

•Teacher has students read a digital selection from The Outsiders and complete a worksheet using Google Docs.

•Teacher has students read a digital selection from The Outsiders. Next students watch a YouTube video covering the selection. Lastly, teacher has a class discussion of the selection and video using Kahoot.

•Teacher assigns a a short video of The Outsiders via YouTube. Next, teacher provides the corresponding text to students via NowComment. Students read the selection, answer questions and participate in an online discussion with other students.

•Teacher has students read a selection from The Outsiders and complete a worksheet using a pencil.

Figure F.4.   Description: ART Model Survey Q4

5.

•Teacher discusses statistics and real world application. Teacher provides students with story problems.

•Teacher provides students with access to TuLyn.com to complete and create statistically based word problems.

•Teacher provides students with a YouTube video of Money Ball covering statistics being used in the real world. Teacher then provides students with statistical questions to answer using Wolframalpha.com.

•Teacher assigns students into teams. Based on the statistics and information gleaned from Moneyball, teams participate in class Fantasy Baseball League (Using fantasysportsmath.com). Teams use known statistical approaches and new approaches to Fantasy League. Students then work in groups and collaborate to create a Prezi explaining their statistical process.

Figure F.5.   Description: ART Model Survey Q5

6.

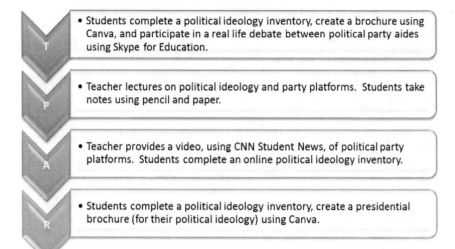

- Students complete a political ideology inventory, create a brochure using Canva, and participate in a real life debate between political party aides using Skype for Education.

- Teacher lectures on political ideology and party platforms. Students take notes using pencil and paper.

- Teacher provides a video, using CNN Student News, of political party platforms. Students complete an online political ideology inventory.

- Students complete a political ideology inventory, create a presidential brochure (for their political ideology) using Canva.

Figure F.6.   Description: ART Model Survey Q6

7.

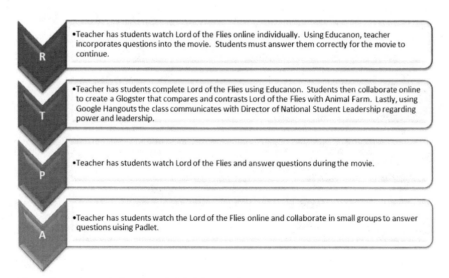

- Teacher has students watch Lord of the Flies online individually. Using Educanon, teacher incorporates questions into the movie. Students must answer them correctly for the movie to continue.

- Teacher has students complete Lord of the Flies using Educanon. Students then collaborate online to create a Glogster that compares and contrasts Lord of the Flies with Animal Farm. Lastly, using Google Hangouts the class communicates with Director of National Student Leadership regarding power and leadership.

- Teacher has students watch Lord of the Flies and answer questions during the movie.

- Teacher has students watch the Lord of the Flies online and collaborate in small groups to answer questions uising Padlet.

Figure F.7.   Description: ART Model Survey Q7

8.

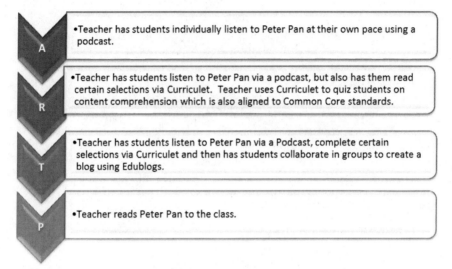

Figure F.8.   Description: ART Model Survey Q8

Look over the previous eight scenarios and write down how many times you circled each letter and complete the following multiplication activity:

P = _____ × 1 = _____
A = _____ × 2 – _____
R = _____ × 3 = _____
T = _____ × 4 = _____

Total = _____

Place an X, corresponding to your total, on the following number grid:

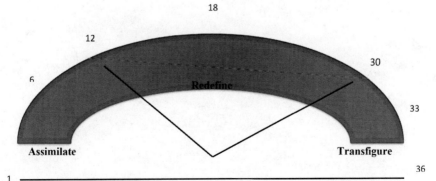

Figure F.9.   Description: ART Model Survey Continuum

The number line above will provide some insight into where each individual falls in his or her technology integration. The chart will help educators understand their current technology integration skill as well as provide a target for moving forward. Using the lesson plan examples as well as the tools offered in Chapter 8 of this book, teachers can begin to develop ideas and lesson plans as well as knowledge of new digital tools to enhance their technology integration.

If a teacher has taken this self-assessment and has scored low in the Transfigure stage, there is still plenty to learn and implement. First, he or she can grow in knowledge of the different digital tools. Second, he or she can work to implement twenty-first-century skills and more cognitive consumption into his or her lesson plans. Lastly he or she can continue to work on providing more *innovative* educational experiences that will ultimately transfigure the classroom.

Bibliography

4 Lessons from K–12 Ed Tech Failures of 2014. Retrieved June 30, 2015, from http://www.centerdigitaled.com/news/4-lessons-from-k-12-ed-tech-failures-of-2014.html.

7 New Educational Web Tools for Teachers—Educational Technology and Mobile Learning. Retrieved July 1, 2015, from http://www.educatorstechnology.com/2015/06/7-new-educational-web-tools-for-teachers.html.

A Global iBook. (2013, January 24). Retrieved from iTunes: https://itunes.apple.com/us/book/a-global-ibook/id710713861?mt=11.

A Must Have Chrome App for Music Teachers. (2015, June 13). Retrieved from Educational Technology and Mobile Learning: http://www.educatorstechnology.com/2015/06/a-must-have-chrome-app-for-music.html.

A Shout Out for Learning Technology's Role in Middle School Student Achievement—NextGen Learning. Retrieved March 31, 2015, from http://nextgenlearning.org/blog/shout-out-learning-technology's-role-middle-school-student-achievement.

Adams, S. (2014). The 10 skills employers most want in 2015 graduates. Retrieved May 28, 2015, from http://www.forbes.com/sites/susanadams/2014/11/12/the-10-skills-employers-most-want-in-2015-graduates/.

Adams, S. (2015). The college degrees and skills employers most want in 2015. Retrieved May 28, 2015, from http://www.forbes.com/sites/susanadams/2015/04/15/the-college-degrees-and-skills-employers-most-want-in-2015/.

Anatomy 4D. (2015, May 27). Retrieved January 18, 2016, from Google Play: https://play.google.com/store/apps/details?id=com.daqri.d4DAnatomy&hl=en.

Aungst, G. (2014, September 4). Using Webb's Depth of Knowledge to increase rigor. Retrieved July 15, 2015, from http://www.edutopia.org/blog/webbs-depth-knowledge-increase-rigor-gerald-aungst.

Barshay, J. (2014, July 29). Why Hoboken is throwing away all of its student laptops. WNYC News. Retrieved from http://www.wnyc.org/story/why -hoboken-throwing-away-all-its-student-laptops/.

Bissonnette, J. D., & Caprino, K. (2014). A call to action research: Action research as an effective professional development model. *Mid-Atlantic Education Review*, 2, 12–22.

Biteslide. (2015, July 7). Retrieved July 9, 2015, from Educational Technology and Mobile Learning: http://www.educatorstechnology.com/2015/07/biteslide -excellent-tool-for-creating-presentations.html.

Bloom, B. S. (1956). *Taxonomy of educational objectives: The classification of educational goals. Handbook 1: Cognitive domain.* New York: McKay.

Blume, H. (2015, January 12). L.A. Unified's iPad program plagued by problems early, review says. *Los Angeles Times, Education.* Retrieved from http://www .latimes.com/local/education/la-me-ipad-report-20150113-story.html.

Book Creator. (2016, January 13). Retrieved January 19, 2016, from iTunes Preview: https://itunes.apple.com/us/app/book-creator-for-ipad-create/ id442378070?mt=8.

Brookhouser, K. (n.d.). How. Retrieved January 20, 2016, from http://www.20time .org/how.

Canva for Education. (2015). Retrieved July 8, 2015, from https://www.canva .com/education/.

CarQuiz Math Game Features and Benefits. Retrieved July 1, 2015, from http:// www.carquizgame.com/features.htm.

Chandler, C. (2015, June 2). Seven tech tools for fast formative assessment. Retrieved January 13, 2016, from MiddleWeb: http://www.middleweb .com/22943/7-tech-tools-for-fast-formative-assessment/.

Christensen Institute. (2015). Our mission. Retrieved January 24, 2016, from Clayton Christensen Institute: http://www.christenseninstitute.org/our-mission/.

Chrome Web Store. (2013, July 7). Retrieved July 15, 2015, from VideoNot.es: https://chrome.google.com/webstore/detail/videonotes/gfpamkcpoehaekol kipeomdbaihfdbdp?hl=en.

Churches, A., Jukes, I., & Crockett, L. *Literacy is not enough: 21st century fluencies for the digital age.* Newbury Park, CA: Corwin, 2011.

Clarisketch—Excellent Tool for Creating Annotated Videos and Sketches—Educational Technology and Mobile Learning. Retrieved July 1, 2015, from http:// www.educatorstechnology.com/2015/06/clarisketch-excellent-tool-for-creat ing-annotated-videos-and-sketches.html.

Clayton Christensen Institute. Retrieved June 15, 2015, from http://www.chris tenseninstitute.org/blended-learning-definitions-and-models/.

Comic & Meme Creator. (2014, June 13). Retrieved July 13, 2015, from Google Play: https://play.google.com/store/apps/details?id=com.tiltedchair.cacomic.

Comic Puppets Lite. (2015, February 8). Retrieved July 13, 2015, from Google Play: https://play.google.com/store/apps/details?id=air.com.touchmultime dia.comicpuppetsfree&hl=en.

Comic Strip It! (lite). (2014, November 9). Retrieved February 22, 2016, from Google Play: https://play.google.com/store/apps/details?id=com.round woodstudios.comicstripit&hl=en.

CrashCourse. (2015, July 20). Retrieved February 22, 2016, from https://www
.youtube.com/user/crashcourse/about.

The Critical 21st Century Skills Every Student Needs and Why. (2015, September). Retrieved May 31, 2015, from http://globaldigitalcitizen.org/critical-21st
-century-skills-every-student-needs.

Curriculet. (2015). Retrieved February 22, 2016, from https://www.curriculet
.com/.

Dangerously Irrelevant. Retrieved March 30, 2015, from http://dangerouslyir
relevant.org/.

Darling-Hammond, L., & Adamson, F. (2014). *Beyond the bubble test: How performance assessments support 21st century learning.* San Francisco: Jossey-Bass.

DepthOfKnowledge_Levels-Definitions-Examples.pdf. Retrieved June 20, 2015,
from http://www.aps.edu/rande/documents/resources/depthofknowledge
_levels-definitions-examples.pdf/view.

Discovery Channel. (2013, September 19). Retrieved July 13, 2015, from Google
Play: https://play.google.com/store/apps/details?id=com.discovery.dsc.

DreamBox Learning. (2014, September). Can technological tools and interventions
boost math achievement? Retrieved March 31, 2015, from http://www.dream
box.com/blog/technological-tools-interventions-boost-math-achievement.

Driving the Skills Agenda. Retrieved June 17, 2015, from http://www.economist
insights.com/analysis/driving-skills-agenda/fullreport.

Duolingo. (2015). Retrieved February 22, 2016, from https://www.duolingo.com/.

Easy Voice Recorder. (2015, March 10). Retrieved July 13, 2015, from Google Play:
https://play.google.com/store/apps/details?id=com.coffeebeanventures
.easyvoicerecorder&hl=en.

Ed Tech Team. (2014, May). 11 fantastic ted ed talks for your students. Retrieved
July 2013, 2015, from Educational Technology and Mobile Learning: http://www
.educatorstechnology.com/2014/05/11-fantastic-ted-ed-talks-for-your.html.

Ed Tech Team. (2015, June 9). Top four presentation tools for teachers. Retrieved
January 14, 2016, from Educational Technology and Mobile Learning: http://
www.educatorstechnology.com/2015/06/top-4-presentation-tools-for-teach
ers.html.

EDpuzzle. (2014, December 7). Retrieved July 15, 2015, from Google Chrome
Store: https://chrome.google.com/webstore/detail/edpuzzle/aibecpgimejiil
codkhopfpbelohhppf?hl=en-US.

Educanon. (2015). Retrieved from https://www.educanon.com/.

Education 2020. (n.d.). Home. Retrieved January 26, 2016, from Education 2020:
https://education-2020.wikispaces.com/.

Educators. (2013). Retrieved July 15, 2015, from ProjectEd: https://www.pro
jected.com/educators.

Educurious. (2015). About Educurious. Retrieved July 15, 2015, from http://edu
curious.org/about/.

Edulastic. (2015). Retrieved July 15, 2015, from http://www.edulastic.com/.

Edusight. Notes. (2015). Retrieved July 1, 2015, from https://edusight.co/notes.

Edutopia. Six examples of iPad integration in the 1:1 classroom. Retrieved March
31, 2015, from http://www.edutopia.org/blog/ipad-integration-classroom
-andrew-marcinek.

Edwards, M. (2014). *Every child, every day: A digital conversion model for student achievement*. Boston, MA: Pearson.

Enyedy, N. (2014). *Personalized Instruction: New interest, old rhetoric, limited results, and the need for a new direction for computer-mediated learning*. Boulder, CO: National Education Policy Center.

Evidence-Based Practices in Online Learning. Retrieved June 15, 2015, from http://www.sri.com/work/projects/evidence-based-practices-online-learning.

Explain Everything Whiteboard. (2016, January 19). Retrieved January 19, 2016, from Chrome Web Store website: https://chrome.google.com/webstore/detail/explain-everything-whiteb/abgfnbfplmdnhfnonljpllnfcobfebag?hl=en.

Feloni, R. (2014). Food network chef Robert Irvine shares the top 5 reasons restaurants fail. Retrieved April 1, 2015, from http://www.businessinsider.com/why-restaurants-fail-so-often-2014-2.

Figurelli, S., & Franzi, N. (2015, August 12). Literacy in the digital age: 5 effective writing tools. Retrieved January 19, 2016, from Teaching Channel: https://www.teachingchannel.org/blog/2015/08/12/literacy-in-the-digital-age-writing- tools-sap/.

Flashcard Hero. (2016, February 12). Retrieved January 15, 2016, from Mac App Store: https://itunes.apple.com/us/app/flashcard-hero-free/id726165621?mt=12.

Ford Model T History and the Early Years of the Ford Motor Company. Retrieved June 3, 2015, from http://www.modelt.ca/background.html.

Four Useful Chromebook Apps for Digital Storytelling. (2015, July 6). Retrieved July 8, 2015, from Educational Technology and Mobile Learning: http://www.educatorstechnology.com/2015/07/4-useful-chromebooks-apps-for-digital-storytelling-on-chromebooks.html.

Free Market Competition in Education Is Good for Economic Growth. Retrieved June 9, 2015, from http://www.ncpa.org/sub/dpd/index.php?article_id=25578.

Future Ready Schools. (2014, July 16). Retrieved from http://www.futureready-schools.org/domain/14.

Garland, S. (2014, May 14). What students really think about technology in the classroom. Retrieved July 9, 2015, from the Hechinger Report: http://hechingerreport.org/students-really-think-technology-classroom/.

Get the Math. (2015). Retrieved from http://www.thirteen.org/get-the-math/.

Glogster Edu. (2015). Retrieved July 2, 2015, from http://webuse.glogster.com/Google.

Google Goggles. (2014, May 28). Retrieved January 15, 2016, from Google Play: https://play.google.com/store/apps/details?id=com.google.android.apps.unveil&hl=en.

Google Hangouts Guide for Teachers. (2015). Retrieved July 15, 2015, from Lee Summit R-7 School District website: https://sites.google.com/a/lsr7.net/hangoutsforteachers/.

Google Slides. (2015). Retrieved from https://www.google.com/slides/about/.

The Great K–12 Debate: Engaging Students with 1:1 and BYOD Initiatives. Retrieved June 30, 2015, from http://www.insight.com/insighton/education/the-great-k12-debate-engaging-students-one-to-one-byod-initiatives.

Guskey, T. (1995). *Professional development in education: New paradigms and practices.* New York: Teacher College Press.

Haiku Jam. (2015). Retrieved from https://edshelf.com/tool/haikujam/.

Halftone 2. (2015, October 29). Retrieved January 18, 2016, from iTunes Preview: https://itunes.apple.com/us/app/halftone-2-comic-book-creator/id603139024?mt=8.

Hanushek, E., & Woessmann, L. (2007). The role of school improvement in economic development. Retrieved February 22, 2016, from http://www.nber.org/papers/w12832.pdf.

Heckman, J. J., & Kautz, T. (2012). Hard evidence on soft skills. *Labour Economics, 19*(4), 451–464.

Heckman, J., & Kautz, T. (2013). Fostering and measuring skills: Interventions that improve character and cognition. Retrieved February 22, 2016, from http://www.nber.org/papers/w19656.

Heckman, J., Stixrud, J., & Urzua, S. (2006). The effects of cognitive and noncognitive abilities on labor market outcomes and social behavior. Retrieved February 22, 2016, from http://www.nber.org/papers/w12006.

Herman, J. L., & Linn, R. L. (2013). *On the road to assessing deeper learning: The status of Smarter Balanced and PARCC assessment consortia.* (CRESST Report 823). Los Angeles, CA: University of California, National Center for Research on Evaluation, Standards, and Student Testing (CRESST).

Hicks, K. (2015, June 4). Top 10 best free math resources on the web. Retrieved January 13, 2016, from http://www.edudemic.com/top-10-free-math-resources-web/.

History in Pictures. (2014, June 5). Retrieved July 13, 2015, from Google Play: https://play.google.com/store/apps/details?id=com.history.in.pics.

Hooker, C. (2015, October 7). Why your 1:1 deployment will fail [Blog post]. Retrieved from HookEd on Innovation: http://hookedoninnovation.com/2013/10/07/why-your-11-deployment-will-fail/.

HSTRY. (2015). Retrieved July 13, 2015, from https://www.hstry.co/features.

Hughes, J., Thomas, R., & Scharber, C. (2006). Assessing technology integration: The RAT—Replacement, Amplification, and Transformation—Framework. In C. Crawford, R. Carlsen, K. McFerrin, J. Price, R. Weber, & D. Willis (Eds.), *Proceedings of Society for Information Technology & Teacher Education International Conference 2006* (pp. 1616–1620). Chesapeake, VA: Association for the Advancement of Computing in Education (AACE).

Human Resources—Professional Development and Evaluation Programs. (2015, January 22). Retrieved July 8, 2015, from Austin Community College: http://www.austincc.edu/hr/profdev/overview.php.

Iasevoli, B. (2013, December 18). After bungled iPad rollout, lessons from LA put tablet technology in a time out. Retrieved June 29, 2015, from The Hechinger Report website: http://hechingerreport.org/after-bungled-ipad-rollout-lessons-from-la-put-tablet-technology-in-a-time-out/.

iBooks Author. (2015, August 30). Retrieved January 19, 2016, from iTunes Preview: https://itunes.apple.com/us/app/ibooks-author/id490152466?mt=12.

Institute for the Future. (2011). Retrieved June 16, 2015, from http://www.iftf.org/futureworkskills/.

International Society for Technology in Education (ISTE). (n.d.). Standards for students. Retrieved January 26, 2016, from ISTE website: http://www.iste.org /standards/iste-standards/standards-for-students.

Irving, W., & Noyik P. (1923). *Rip van Vinkl: di legende fun farshlofenem tol.* New York: Farlag H. Toybenshlag.

iTunes Preview. (2013, February 4). Retrieved July 1, 2015, from Davinci Note: https://itunes.apple.com/us/app/davinci-note/id571886658?mt=8.

Kahoot! (2014, July 9). Retrieved from Google Play: https://play.google.com /store/apps/details?id=no.mobitroll.kahoot.android&hl=en.

Kaizena. About. (2015). Retrieved July 15, 2015, from https://kaizena.com/about.

Khan Academy. (2015). Retrieved from https://www.khanacademy.org/.

Khan Academy. (2016, January 8). Retrieved January 15, 2016, from Wikipedia: https://en.wikipedia.org/wiki/Khan_Academy.

Koehler, M. (2011, May 13). What is TPACK? Retrieved January 24, 2016, from http://www.tpack.org/.

Krathwhol, D. R. (2002). A revision of Bloom's Taxonomy: An overview. *Theory Into Practice, 41*(4). Retrieved from http://www.unco.edu/cetl/sir/stating _outcome/documents/Krathwohl.pdf.

Last Day of Model T Production at Ford. Retrieved June 4, 2015, from http:// www.history.com/this-day-in-history/last-day-of-model-t-production-at-ford.

Late Nineteenth and Early Twentieth-Century Economic Trends. Retrieved June 3, 2015, from http://www.westga.edu/~hgoodson/economic trends.htm.

Learn World History. (2015, January 6). Retrieved July 13, 2015, from Google Play: https://play.google.com/store/apps/details?id=com.ma.ld.dict.history.

Learning with 'e's. Retrieved May 27, 2015, from http://steve-wheeler.blogspot .com/.

Livingston, P. (2014). What failing restaurants can tell us about 1-to-1. Retrieved February 17, 2016, from http://pamelalivingston.com/2014/09/what-can-fail ing-restaurants-tell-us-about-1-to-1/.

Marshall, J. (2015). www.Quickanddirtytips.com/math-dude. Retrieved July 1, 2015, from Math Dude.

MathsFrame. (2012). Retrieved from http://mathsframe.co.uk/.

Means, B., Toyama, Y., Murphy, R., Bakia, M., & Jones, K. (2010). *Evaluation of evidence-based practices in online learning: A meta-analysis and review of online learning studies.* Washington, DC: U.S. Department of Education.

Merriam-Webster. Retrieved June 3, 2015, from http://www.merriam-webster. com/dictionary/rote; http://www.merriam-webster.com/dictionary/assimi late; http://www.merriam-webster.com/dictionary/redesign; http://www .merriam-webster.com/dictionary/transfigure.

Mizerny, C. (2014, December 07). Students often prefer low tech learning. Retrieved July 9, 2015, from http://www.middleweb.com/19276/low-tech -teaching/.

Nearpod. (2015). Retrieved February 22, 2016, from https://www.nearpod.com/.

Newsela. (2014, April 29). Retrieved July 15, 2015, from Google Chrome Webstore: https://chrome.google.com/webstore/detail/newsela/bfpeiapdhnegnfcfkdfi habadngjagfj?hl=en-US.

Ng, P. T. (2007). Educational reform in Singapore: From quantity to quality. *Educational Research for Policy and Practice, 7*(1), 5–15.

Nichols, J. R. (2013, March 4). 8 educational apps to create digital portfolio. Retrieved from http://www.teachthought.com/technology/8-educational-apps-to-create-digital-portfolios/.

NowComment.com. Retrieved July 1, 2015, from http://nowcomment.com/.

One to One Institute. Retrieved June 29, 2015, from http://www.one-to-oneinstitute.org/.

OpenSchool ePortfolio. (2014, December 16). Retrieved from Google Play: https://play.google.com/store/apps/details?id=com.openschool.app&hl=en.

Overview of Google Docs, Sheets, and Slides. (2015). Retrieved July 13, 2015, from Google: https://support.google.com/docs/answer/49008?hl=en.

Padlet. (2015, March 22). Retrieved January 13, 2016, from Chrome Web Store: https://chrome.google.com/webstore/detail/padlet/ppckapbnfhikdajgehibja pcohbaomhd?hl=en.

Papert, S., & Caperton, G. (1999). Vision for education: The Caperton-Papert platform. Retrieved July 8, 2015, from http://www.papert.org/articles/Vision _for_education.html.

Partnership for 21st Century Learning. Retrieved April 1, 2015, from http://www .p21.org/.

Payne, J., Griffin, B., McCaffrey, D., Karam, R., Daugherty, L., & Phillips, A. (2013). Research brief: Does an algebra course with tutoring software improve student learning (Issue Brief No. RB-9746-DEIES). Retrieved February 22, 2016, from RAND Corporation http://www.rand.org/pubs/research_briefs /RB9746.html.

PBS. (2015). Retrieved July 1, 2015, from http://www.pbslearningmedia.org/.

Permission Click. (2015). Retrieved July 13, 2015, from https://www.permission click.com/.

Peterson, P., & Horn, M. (2016). The ideal blended learning combination. *Education Next, 16*(2). Retrieved February 22, 2016, from http://educationnext.org/ideal-blended-learning-combination-instructional-computer-time/.

Pink, D. H. (2009). *Drive: The surprising truth about what motivates us.* New York: Riverhead Books.

PISA 2012 Results—OECD. Retrieved June 24, 2015, from http://www.oecd.org /pisa/keyfindings/pisa-2012-results.htm.

Postman, N. (1985). *Amusing ourselves to death: Public discourse in the age of show business.* London: Penguin Books.

Presentious. (2015). Retrieved February 22, 2016, from https://presentio.us/.

Project Tomorrow—Home. Retrieved June 15, 2015, from http://www.tomorrow .org/.

Purpose Games. (2015). Retrieved July 13, 2015, from http://www.purpose games.com/create.

Quiver. (2015). Retrieved February 22, 2016, from https://edshelf.com/tool /quiver/.

QuotesCover. (2015). Retrieved July 1, 2015, from QuotesCover: http://www .quotescover.com/.

Read&Write for Google. (2015, June 12). Retrieved from Chrome Web Store: https://chrome.google.com/webstore/detail/readwrite-for-google/inoeonmf apjbbkmdafoankkfajkcphgd?hl=en-US.

Rip Van Winkle. Retrieved March 30, 2015, from http://en.wikipedia.org/wiki/rip_van_winkle.

ScribbleMaps. (2015). Retrieved January 17, 2016, from http://www.scribble maps.com/.

Seesaw: Student driven digital portfolios. (n.d.). Retrieved January 19, 2016, from http://web.seesaw.me/.

Shockley, S. (2015, May 19). A teen take on ed tech. Retrieved July 9, 2015, from Huffington Post: http://www.huffingtonpost.com/youth-radio-youth-media -international/a-teen-take-on-edtech_b_7336854.html.

Skype for Education. (2015). Retrieved July 15, 2015, from https://education .skype.com/.

Smithsonian Channel. (2015, June 4). Retrieved July 13, 2015, from Google Play: https://play.google.com/store/apps/details?id=com.smithsonian.android.

Socrative. (2015). Retrieved July 8, 2015, from http://socrative.com/.

Standards for Professional Learning. (n/a). Retrieved July 8, 2015, from Learning Forward: http://learningforward.org/docs/pdf/standardsreferenceguide .pdf?sfvrsn=0.

Steckner, S. (2015, April 5). The great K–12 debate: Engaging students with 1:1 and BYOD initiatives. Insight. Retrieved February 22, 2016, from http://www .insight.com/insighton/education/the-great-k12-debate-engaging-students -one-to-one-byod-initiatives/.

Stone, B. (2015). *Things a little birdie told me: Creative secrets from the cofounder of Twitter.* New York: Grand Central Publishing.

Strauss, V. (2014, February 28). A video that shows why teachers are going out of their minds. Retrieved July 8, 2015, from the Washington Post: http://www .washingtonpost.com/blogs/answer-sheet/wp/2014/02/28/a-video-that -shows-why-teachers-are-going-out-of-their-minds/?tid=pm_pop.

Study.com. (2010, January 26). New study links education to economic growth [Blog post]. Retrieved from Education Insider News Blog: http://study.com /articles/New_Study_Links_Education_to_Economic_Growth.html.

Tape-a-Talk. (2014, May 21). Retrieved July 13, 2015, from Google Play: https://play.google.com/store/apps/details?id=name.markus.droesser.tape atalk&hl=en.

Taylor, F. W. (1919). *The principles of scientific management.* New York, NY: Harper & Brothers Publisher.

Technology and Student Achievement—The Right Question to Ask. Retrieved March 31, 2015, from https://www.clarity-innovations.com/blog/tjohnston /technology-and-student-achievement-right-question-ask.

Technology Is Learning. (n.d.). SAMR model. Retrieved January 24, 2016, from Technology Is Learning: https://sites.google.com/a/msad60.org/technology -is-learning/samr-model.

TED-Ed. (2015). Retrieved from http://ed.ted.com/about.

Teens and Technology 2013. (2013, December). Retrieved March 30, 2015, from http://www.pewinternet.org/2013/03/13/teens-and-technology-2013/.

Telese, J. A. (2012). Middle school mathematics teachers' professional development and student achievement. *Journal of Educational Research, 105,* 102–111.

Tellagami Edu. (2015). Retrieved July 2, 2015, from https://tellagami.com/edu/.

The Answer Pad. (2015). Retrieved from https://theanswerpad.com/.

The Getty. (2015). Retrieved July 13, 2015, from http://www.getty.edu/about /opencontent.html.

Things you should know about . . . Flipped classrooms [White paper]. (2012, February). Retrieved November 15, 2015, from Educause: https://net.educause.edu/ir /library/pdf/ELI7081.pdf.

Three Ring. (2015, June 10). Retrieved July 13, 2015, from iTunes: https://itunes .apple.com/us/app/three-ring/id504311049?mt=8&ign-mpt=uo%3D8.

Twiducate. (2012). Retrieved July 13, 2015, from http://www.twiducate.com/.

United States Constitution. (2012, April 6). Retrieved July 13, 2015, from Google Play: https://play.google.com/store/apps/details?id=com.hotrod.reference .spiritofseventysix.

Using Webb's Depth of Knowledge to Increase Rigor. (2014, September 14). Retrieved June 21, 2015, from http://www.edutopia.org/blog/webbs-depth -knowledge-increase-rigor-gerald-aungst.

VideoNot.es. (2013, July 7). Retrieved June 5, 2016, from Google Chrome Web Store website: https://chrome.google.com/webstore/detail/videonotes/gfpa mkcpoehaekolkipeomdbaihfdbdp?hl=en.

Visme. (2015). Retrieved July 1, 2015, from Visme: http://www.visme.co/.

Wang, M. C., Haertel, G. D., & Walberg, H. J. (1997). *What helps students learn?* Philadelphia, PA: Mid-Atlantic Regional Educational Laboratory.

We Learned It. (2015, June 10). Retrieved July 15, 2015, from iTunes: https:// itunes.apple.com/us/app/welearnedit/id906780940?mt=8.

Webbs DOK Guide. Retrieved June 20, 2015, from http://www.aps.edu/rande /documents/resources/webbs_dok_guide.pdf/view.

Wendt, S., Rice, J., & Nokamoto, J. (2014, October). Evaluation of the MIND Re-search Institute's Spatial Temporal Math program in California. Retrieved from http://www.wested.org/wp-content/2007files_mf/1415730200Evaluation _STMath_Program_20141111.pdf.

Wiggins, G. (2011, June). The student voice, part 5—common practices that don't work. Retrieved March 30, 2015, from https://grantwiggins.wordpress .com/2011/12/06/the-student-voice-our-survey-part-5-common-practices -that-dont-work/.

Wlodarz, D. (2013). 7 big mistakes K–12 education needs to avoid in 1:1 com-puting plans. Beta News. Retrieved February 22, 2016, from http://betanews .com/2013/07/22/7-big-mistakes-k-12-education-needs-to-avoid-in-11-com puting-plans/.

World Map 2015. (2015). Retrieved July 13, 2015, from Google Play: https://play .google.com/store/apps/details?id=com.appventions.worldmapfree&hl=en.

You Are the Essence of Learning, Not a School or University—Big Think. (2015). Retrieved March 30, 2015, from http://bigthink.com/think-tank/you-are-the -essence-of-learning-not-a-school-or-university.

YummyMath. (2015). Retrieved February 22, 2016, from http://www.yummy math.com/.

ZeeMaps. (2015). Retrieved February 22, 2016, from https://www.zeemaps.com/

About the Author

Dr. Michael Martin currently serves as the high school principal for Buckeye Central Local Schools in New Washington, Ohio. He proudly serves the institution that represents his alma mater. At Buckeye Central he is beginning to spearhead the district's digital conversion.

Following graduation from Heidelberg University, he began his education career at the First Church of God in Toledo, Ohio. He then moved to Millbury-Lake School District where he served as a history teacher and basketball coach. He then made stops at Cardington-Lincoln and Plymouth High Schools before moving into his first administrative role at Pioneer Career & Technology Center.

He received a degree in history and an alias in philosophy and political science. He pursued a degree in social studies at Toledo University before settling on a master's in business administration from Tiffin University. After completing his MBA, he realized his future was in education and not basketball, leading him to complete his doctoral degree in educational leadership from Ashland University.

He is considered an innovator in technology integration as well as an expert in the field of professional development and classroom instruction. As such, he has had the opportunity to serve as an adjunct professor as well as an educational consultant. He has a busy speaking schedule and has made numerous national, state, and local presentations.

He has a passion for his work and service in education but humbly realizes his real purpose in life is to serve God and the world as well as to lead his household as a husband to one and a father of four. He resides with his wife and four beautiful daughters in Willard, Ohio.